Go MAD
the art of
making a
difference

D1439782

Copyright © 2005 Andy Gilbert

The rights of Andy Gilbert to be identified as the author of this work have been asserted in accordance with the Copyright, Designs and Patents Act 1988.

First published in Great Britain in 1999 by:
Go MAD Books
Pocket Gate Farm
Off Breakback Road
Woodhouse Eaves
Leicestershire
LE12 8RS

All rights reserved. No part of this publication may be reproduced, stored in a retrieval system, or transmitted in any form or by any means without the prior written consent of the publisher.

ISBN 0-9543292-6-0

British Library Cataloguing in Publication Data.
A catalogue record for this book is available from the British Library.

Printed and bound in Great Britain by
Biddles Ltd, Norfolk

Go MAD® is a registered trademark

This book is dedicated to people of all ages.

Most importantly…

To those who want to increase their ability to make a difference – however large or small.
Whatever you choose, you can Go MAD

Secondly…

To those who continually make a difference in whatever they do.
Thank you for inspiring others to greater success. Keep on being the difference that makes a difference.

And finally…

To those who are unhappy with their current situation and perhaps believe others are to blame.
This is your chance to take responsibility and do something positive. Discover how you can make a difference.

Go MAD

Go MAD® /go mad/v.,n., & adj. abbr. Go Make A Difference. A solution focused thinking system designed to add value to any individual and to any organisation in achieving any difference that they want to make through: greater clarity of thinking; increased speed of thinking; improved creative thinking; to achieve consistency in achieving personal and business goals. Measured business improvement by the structured development and application of people's ability to Make A Difference.

Contents

PRINCIPLE FOUR: HAVE SELF-BELIEF THAT YOU CAN AND WILL MAKE A DIFFERENCE

PRINCIPLE FIVE: INVOLVE OTHERS TO HELP YOU GO MAD

PRINCIPLE SIX: TAKE PERSONAL RESPONSIBILITY FOR YOUR ACTIONS

PRINCIPLE SEVEN: TAKE ACTION AND MEASURE THE RESULTS

GO MAD ABOUT THINKING – APPLYING GO MAD AS A SOLUTION FOCUSED THINKING SYSTEM

FINAL THOUGHTS – THE BIT AT THE END

"**We all live with the objective of being happy;
our lives are all different and yet the same.**"
Anne Frank

INTRODUCTION

1. The Start Of Something

Hello... and welcome to Go MAD – *The Art of Making A Difference.*

The secret of making a difference is that there is no secret. There are only successful principles, which anyone can apply. The information and principles contained within this book will change your life, if you choose to apply them. I know, because what you are about to read has already changed my life and the lives of many others.

Whatever your reason for reading this book, my aim is to help you understand and develop your ability to make a difference. Any difference, big or small, that you consider being worthwhile. *Making a difference* is not just about doing something differently or for the first time. It is also about making improvements and building on that which already exists.

I'm not going to beat around the bush. If you want to make a difference, this book will definitely help. If you don't, then that's fine. Have a browse through the pages and then give the book to someone who does want to make a difference. Alternatively, put it somewhere safe for some future moment when you decide you do want to Go MAD.

Now, if you want to save yourself a couple of minutes reading time, I suggest you skip over the next few pages. I'm about to share with you the background behind this book, the research undertaken and how to get the most from reading it. If you don't want to know this, please turn to the section entitled *Getting Straight to the Point.*

2. Ruts And Dreams

In 1996 I was in a rut. A career rut. Feeling let down and trapped inside a company where the short-term objectives and behaviour of the directors conflicted with my personal values. It was, however, a comfortable rut – one I had started getting used to – with a nice car, good salary, pleasant working conditions and friendly colleagues who respected my expertise and contribution to the business. Nevertheless, it was a rut and one I needed to escape from.

In November 1996, I completed the dissertation of my Masters Degree in Human Resource Development. It focused on how people managed their careers – or rather didn't, in the majority of cases. I realised that whilst I knew the theory of career management, and had helped many others with their careers, I was not applying it to myself. I concluded that I needed to align the work I did in the future with my values. I made the decision to leave my full-time job and establish a values-driven training and development consultancy. Six weeks later I escaped from the rut and formed my first company, Career Strategies Ltd, as a vehicle for my dreams.

3. Purpose And Passion

It was a great career decision. I had previously gained considerable experience as a consultant in a large-scale organisational change and restructuring. I specialised in helping companies develop ways of managing people issues and optimising employee reaction to change. My work now involved using my training and development expertise to design and deliver training and personal development programmes for a growing number of organisations affected by change. I enjoyed the variety of my work in training managers, developing teams and coaching individuals.

My company grew and I was passionate about the projects and people I was working with. However, I realised that I needed to communicate my values to others more clearly. I struggled, like many organisations do, to write a meaningful mission statement; without a great deal of success. I mentioned this to my personal coach, Tim, who suggested that I write a "passion statement" instead.

"What's one of those?" I asked.

"I don't know," he replied, "I just made it up!"

"Well, what should it look like?" I asked, naively.

"I don't know, I've never seen one." Tim stated rather obviously.

So I wrote a list of things I felt passionate about, shared it with the team, gained their input and produced the world's first company passion statement.

Being the brightness is one step beyond seeing the light. To be passionate about opening minds, encouraging development, gaining insight, exploring parameters, igniting desires, harnessing energy, inspiring people, moving forward, increasing skills, sowing thoughts, achieving goals, reviewing effectiveness, releasing potential, facing fears, generating happiness, taking responsibility, enjoying learning, overcoming obstacles, building teams, facilitating success, having fun, getting started, believing in choices, being the brightness and **making a difference**. *The answers are on the inside.*

The significance of this statement is twofold. Firstly, it describes the way the company operates both internally and externally. Secondly, it brought the phrase *making a difference* into our day-to-day activities – which ultimately led to the abbreviation M.A.D. and changing the company name to Go MAD.

4. The Meaning Of Words And The Making Of Decisions

Months later, one of the team, Kathryn Roberts, asked me what I thought *making a difference* really meant. We started to bounce ideas around about how some people succeeded in what they set out to achieve and why others didn't. We speculated about the essential elements of how to make a difference and after several enjoyable, but inconclusive, hours we made an important decision. We needed evidence. The decision was made to undertake a 12 month research project to identify the key principles applied when people were successful in making a difference.

We needed to decide who would conduct the research and how it would be done. It was now December 1997. One year had passed and the company was making a profit. By this time, I had already decided to contribute over 50% of the company's first year profits to a worthwhile educational development project. Three months previously I had offered to pay the salary and expenses of a school mathematics teacher (Ian Chakravorty) for a one-year secondment. This was an opportune coincidence. I believed Ian would be the ideal person to conduct the research, with his detailed analytical skills and desire to make a difference in educating others. We agreed that whatever the results of the research, we would endeavour to make the findings accessible within schools and for the benefit of young people.

5. The Original Research Question

In January 1998, we started. Adopting, what researchers call, a phenomenological approach (i.e. studying the phenomenon of making a difference), our original research question was, **"What is the simplest way of explaining the success process that people naturally use when making a difference?"** (What we discovered was not a process, but a thinking system. However, more about that later.) Ian, armed with a tape-recorder and notepad, set off around the U.K. to interview people who had made a difference. I initially introduced Ian to three people, whom I considered had made a difference, for him to interview. They each introduced Ian to three further people, whom they considered had made a difference, whom in turn provided similar introductions. Other people were interviewed as a result of reading or hearing about the differences they had made.

There were no criteria for specifying what the difference should be. Hence, these differences encompassed a wide range of successful activities: commercial, career, balanced lifestyle, political, family, community, educational, personal relationships and many more. Some differences were on a large scale, others much smaller. All were significant to the individuals making the difference.

Meanwhile, Kathryn and I headed up a team of eight consultants researching the differences made by individuals in the workplace. A variety of organisations from the public, private and voluntary sectors were invited to nominate individuals who had made a difference. The range of occupations was diverse and included people of all ages and levels within the organisations. The differences they had made included: doubling the sales turnover of a company; providing exceptional customer care; increasing production by 100%; managing organisational change; enhancing their career; developing others; and implementing a variety of cost saving initiatives. For two months we filmed each research interview we conducted. We wanted to understand the key success principles which were commonly being applied in order to achieve results.

"I do whatever I can, wherever I can, whenever I can, for as long as I can, with whatever I have, to make a difference."
Jimmy Carter

Go MAD – the art of making a difference

By the end of the year we had gathered collectively an incredible amount of information from a diverse range of sources, all of which related to how individuals successfully made a difference. We continually re-listened to each taped interview, analysed the film footage and studied relevant background reading material. From all of this, emerged *Go MAD – The Art of Making A Difference*; a practical and easily understandable framework for success comprising seven key principles.

During the latter part of 1998 and early 1999, we tested the Go MAD Principles in a variety of ways. Ian ran pilot Go MAD development programmes in schools for students and teachers. Kathryn and I delivered Go MAD development and coaching programmes for managers. We began helping more and more people to consciously apply the seven key principles and started to realise that the Go MAD principles could be applied to anything to increase the probability of success – business improvement, sporting performance, health and fitness, education, financial security, career development – the list is endless.

6. Six Years Later Plus A Breakthrough In Thinking

This book was originally published in October 1999 following the completion of the initial research in February of the same year. 70,000 books and 6 years later it was time to update the original with a revised second edition.

So much has happened as a result of the development and application of the Go MAD Framework – which you are about to discover – which I did not forsee when it was developed in 1999. My life has changed considerably, travelling around the world developing people and businesses from over 30 countries in the use of Go MAD. Plus, building a great team of Go MAD "Thinking Engineers" has enabled me to impact the lives of tens of thousands of people who have consciously applied the key principles I discovered successful people were naturally using to make a difference. Whilst these key principles and the Go MAD Framework remain exactly the same, the applications of these to achieve personal and business success have been so amazing – both in results and diversity – that I sometimes struggle to keep track.

Each year I continue to write one or two books, in addition to my research and consulting activities, focusing on how to apply Go MAD, as a solution focused approach to a range of specific business and personal issues. Books relating to Coaching, Leadership, Organisational Change, Meetings, Negotiating, Career Management, Customer Care and Optimising Your Brain represent just eight of the specific areas I have focused on since writing this book. My list of over 30 Go MAD applications continues to grow and will ensure I keep busy!

As the use of the Go MAD Framework has grown over the years, I have had several major realisations. Firstly, that Go MAD is not a process but a system comprised of interdependent components and understanding the relationship between them is as important as applying each of the key principles. Secondly, that whilst the Framework can be understood and applied very easily by almost everyone at a personal level, there are more in-depth applications for large-scale change and business improvement programmes. "Structured commonsense" and, "Simple, yet sophisticated" are two phrases that many people use to describe Go MAD. The third, and most important, realisation provided a major breakthrough in the way that the Go MAD Framework is applied – using it as a "Thinking System". Now, before I get too carried away explaining lots of interesting and useful information about how our thinking affects our ability to obtain results, it is important to remind myself of the reason for sharing this with you. As I became totally immersed in the Go MAD research and the various applications to help people develop their thinking and businesses improve their performance, I realised I had discovered my true purpose in life. My primary aim had become, and still is:

"Helping people to understand and develop their ability to make a difference."

Twelve words which describe not only my personal passion, but also the purpose of this book. So whatever personal or business success you are seeking to achieve my intent is to help you. However, in doing so I have to recognise that different people have different levels of ability. This book was originally written in line with my primary aim. What I now realise is that this is just an introduction to understanding and applying Go MAD at a personal effectiveness level. However, if you are already achieving the success you aspire to at a personal level – in all areas of your life – you may wish to make a difference by helping others, teams or organisations to achieve the differences important to them. To do so, then a deeper or more specialist understanding can be gained by studying one of the more recent books I have written (visit the website www.gomadthinking.com for an up to date list of publications) or learning advanced Solution Focused Thinking skills by attending a Go MAD development programme.

However, as you are currently reading this book, I thought that what might be helpful is to give you an insight into how the Go MAD Framework is being used as a thinking system – to help both individuals and organisations develop and achieve greater results on a daily basis. Hence, in this second edition of the book, I have included a new final section which will hopefully serve as an introduction to Solution Focused Thinking and wider applications of Go MAD as a thinking system.

7. Getting The Most From This Book

This book is for everyone: for people of all ages and in all walks of life; for students and chief executives; for those leaving school to work; for those leaving work to retire; for those at work; and for those not working. For many people, it is likely to be the first personal development book they will read. If this is not the case for you then I believe you will find the content practical and perhaps easier to apply than many of the other books you might already have read.

Whatever your background and current situation, the following points are offered to help you maximise the differences you make during and after reading this book.

- Read the next section *Getting Straight To The Point,* even if you read nothing else. It summarises the research findings by outlining the seven key principles and explaining how Go MAD can be used as a thinking system to help you successfully make the differences you desire.

- The rest of the book is divided into seven sections that explain the seven key principles in greater detail. Each section is broken down into several mini-chapters, as most people seem to prefer bite-size chunks of information.

- As you continue reading, you will find that this book is written in a pretty informal way. I will share examples, both successful and otherwise, of how others and myself have attempted to Go MAD, together with the lessons learned.

- You will also discover I can be quite direct at times – by just giving you the facts and challenging you to apply them. This book does not aim to provide you with an in-depth theoretical description of underpinning psychological reasoning. Instead it provides the essential information in an easy to understand format that you can practically apply.

- Each section includes a selection of my favourite inspirational quotes to reinforce the key principles. They are from a variety of sources, including some of my own. You don't have to agree with each one, just give them some thought. For example:

**"It is not the mountain we conquer,
but ourselves."
Sir Edmund Hillary**

- A variety of questions and exercises are included for you to consider. You obviously don't have to complete these. Unless of course you are serious about *really* wanting to make a difference. You should, however, **be aware that completing the exercises will seriously increase your ability to make a difference**. I recognise that some people prefer not to write in a book, in case someone else reads it. If this is a concern of yours, then use a separate piece of paper.

- I encourage you to write in this book. However, I realise this might be difficult at first, particularly if you had a mother like mine. I remember being told, for very practical reasons, not to write in books or fold the corners of pages, because the books did not belong to me. Well this book is yours to keep. So write in it, even if you only do it in pencil. Underline words, make notes and highlight sections that seem important.

- Let's find out how easy this is. Imagine that you have been asked to compile a dictionary. You're up to the letter S and are about to define the word "success."

Complete the following definition in your own words.

Success is .....

Please complete this exercise before you continue reading. It is there for a purpose, which will be revealed later in the book.

- Read with a purpose. Identify something in your life you want to make a difference about and apply what you read to this difference.

- Adopt a supermarket shopping trolley approach. By this, I mean look for what you want and like. Different people want different things. There is plenty of information in this book, but not everyone will want everything. Only put the ideas in your trolley that you want to use. When you reread this book, you will notice different things that you didn't take from the shelf previously.

**"Choice, not chance,
determines the difference you make."
Andy Gilbert**

Complete the exercises. I mentioned this earlier, but thought it needed emphasising once more. Have you defined success yet? In order to gain the greatest benefit from this book, I suggest you first read it from cover to cover. Then treat it as an active book, not a passive one – use it; don't just read it. Each time you decide to Go MAD about something, revisit each section and take the necessary action. I hope you will find it useful to refer to throughout your life.

So now, get on with it and get stuck in. Enjoy what you discover.

Go on.......Go MAD

Andy Gilbert

**"There is nothing brilliant
nor outstanding in my record,
except perhaps this one thing:
I do the things that I believe
ought to be done...
and when I make up my mind to do a thing,
I act."
Theodore Roosevelt**

GETTING STRAIGHT
TO THE POINT

8. First, The Good News

Anyone can make a difference. A high I.Q. or evidence of academic ability is not an essential requirement. Whilst both might be useful in gaining employment, I have discovered no evidence linking either with the ability to make a difference. There is hope for us all!

9. The Seven Key Principles

1. Have a **strong reason why** you want to make a difference.
2. **Define your goal** before starting to make a difference.
3. Consider possibilities and **plan your priorities** before taking action to make a difference.
4. Have **self-belief** that you can and will make a difference.
5. **Involve others** to help you make a difference.
6. **Take personal responsibility** for your actions.
7. **Take action** and measure the results of the difference you make.

Principle 1 considers WHY you want to make a difference.
Principle 2 focuses on WHAT difference you want to make.
Principles 3-7 concentrate on HOW to make the difference.

We identified that individuals who were successful in making a difference, regardless of what that difference was, had applied these principles. However, we also discovered a relationship between these key principles that is equally important to understand. This is illustrated in the next section.

10. Go MAD – The Framework

The pyramid diagram is useful in understanding the importance of the seven key principles and the critical links between them. It also provides a simple framework with which to consciously apply the principles.

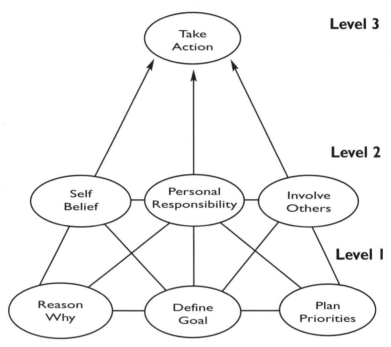

The Go MAD® Framework

Notice the three levels of the pyramid. The first level we refer to as **personal planning** and it links principles one, two and three. These are the foundations upon which success is built. It takes a **strong reason why** (principle one) to maintain motivation, face challenges and overcome obstacles. Hence, this is a cornerstone. The other cornerstone is provided by a well constructed **plan of priorities** (principle three). These principles are linked by having a **defined goal** (principle two) to centrally support the remaining four principles.

Priorities cannot be planned without a defined goal, and the goal cannot be achieved without a strong enough reason to make a difference. With these foundations in place, a second level can be built.

The second level we refer to as **maintaining momentum** and this builds upon the personal planning of the foundation level. Having the **self-belief** (principle four) to succeed in making a difference is dependent upon having a defined goal which, you believe, is possible to achieve. Without the self-belief and the desire to achieve, progress will falter. Hence, the link with having a strong enough reason to make a difference.

Involving others (principle five) should be built into the plan and prioritised. Before doing this, a key aspect of planning priorities (principle 3) is to engage in possibility thinking and consider options. The defined goal and plan of priorities established at the foundation level will need to be communicated and both might need to be revised following the involvement of others. Without this involvement and the additional support this brings, it might be impossible to move to the next level.

At the centre of the Go MAD Framework is the choice every individual has of taking **personal responsibility** for their actions (principle six) to make a difference. If this choice is exercised then the other key principles, with which it links, stand a chance of being applied. However, in order to move to the third level all of the first six principles have to be in place.

The third level is that of **making a difference** and can only be reached by building the foundations with the first three principles and maintaining the momentum by applying principles four, five and six. Even then, it is still necessary to **take action** and measure the results (principle seven) to know that the goal has been achieved and a difference has been made.

"To accomplish great things we must not only act, but also dream; not only plan, but also believe."
Anatole France

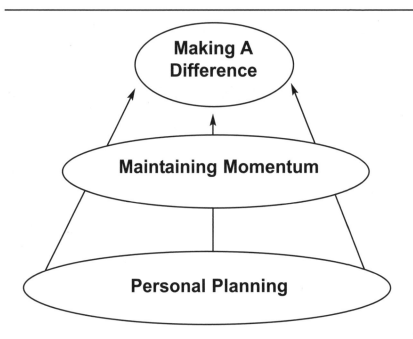

11. More Good News

You are already successful in applying these key principles – at least some of the time. Let me give you a simple example of how you apply them on a daily basis.

Think about travelling to get somewhere. There is always a reason why you get out of bed in the morning. Sometimes the reason is because you want to do something and it is strong enough to get you up instantly; perhaps the thought of an important or enjoyable event e.g. going on holiday. At other times, after temporarily delaying the start of the day with the alarm snooze button, the main reason to get up is often linked with not wanting something to happen. For example, the fear of upsetting others, embarrassment of being late or the consequences of losing a job. Either way, whether the reason is towards or away from motivation, it is strong enough to cause you to get out of bed.

Your defined goal (principle two) might be to get to a place by a specific time. In order to do this you will have considered the possibilities, prioritised (principle three) what needs to be done and allowed sufficient time to do it. This might include preparing clothes to wear, washing, eating, exercising, packing, travelling, etc. You have probably involved others (principle five) in elements of the planning, preparation or travelling to your destination. You believe it is achievable to get there on time (principle four) and the responsibility for doing so is yours (principle six). You travel, arrive, check your watch and measure the results of your actions (principle seven).

12. A Sad Reality

Many people successfully apply these key principles day to day without consciously thinking about them. Most people arrive at work or school on time; they complete their shopping, and undertake a wide range of activities that could all be classed as making a difference. However, in my experience of working with thousands of people in many organisations, most people do not apply these key principles consistently. What's more, the majority of people employed do not appear to believe in their own ability to make a difference or take responsibility for doing so. Quite often people find themselves in an environment where the prevailing culture is: "Do as you're told," or, "Do as we've always done." Hence, there is a lack of encouragement for individuals to make a difference and their ability to do so, is stifled.

"Where there's no will... there's no way!"
Andy Gilbert

Many times when delivering development programmes, I have

Go MAD – the art of making a difference

discovered people who make an incredible difference outside of work – at home, in the community and with social activities – but choose not to apply the seven key principles in the workplace. This can lead to feelings of frustration or helplessness; an atmosphere of blame: "It's the manager's fault," and becoming stuck in a rut.

The sad reality is that it is easier to place the blame with others rather than taking personal responsibility for making a difference.

If you want to make a difference, whether it be at work or elsewhere in your life, you need to take responsibility and consciously apply the Go MAD key principles.

13. Making A Start

Take a few seconds to think about your life. How is it progressing so far? What would you like to change or improve? What would you like to have more or less of? What areas would you possibly like to make a difference about? The following list is provided to stimulate your thinking about possible areas:

- an aspect of work
- fitness
- learning
- developing skills
- certain projects
- financial situation
- friendships
- reading
- health
- career development
- decorating/D.I.Y.

- education
- relationships
- balanced lifestyle
- watching less T.V.
- sport
- social activities
- customers
- relaxation
- local community
- increasing knowledge
- what else?

TIME TO WRITE

Make a note of at least a couple of areas that you might want to Go MAD about. This involves writing them down - but only if you *really* want to get the most from this book!

Keep these areas in mind as you continue to read about each key principle. Apply the detailed information in each section to the areas that you want to make a difference about. By doing this, you will notice that by the end of the book you will have dramatically improved your probability of making the differences you truly desire.

**"You see things and say, 'Why?' but I dream
things that never were and say, 'Why not?' "
George Bernard Shaw**

Principle One

HAVE A STRONG

REASON WHY

YOU WANT TO

GO MAD

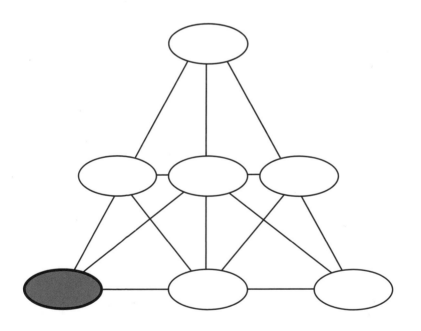

"**A person can bear any what,
if they have a big enough why.
He who has a why to live for,
can bear almost any how.**"
Frederick Nietsche

14. New Year Resolutions And Whining Dogs

At 11.45 p.m. each December 31st, with a drink in one hand and the other clutching a handful of crisps, millions of people talk about differences they intend to make. Differences that, for most, will not be made! New Year's Eve is absolutely the wrong time of year to decide to make a difference. For the next few weeks, membership of health and fitness clubs increase, habits temporarily halt and what's the reason why? "It's my New Year resolution!" Very often, this tradition at New Year is the only reason why and, for most people, it does not prove to be strong enough as a motive for continued action.

Now imagine a scene from an American movie, set in an old mid-western town. There is a house with a large wooden porch and a rocking chair for Grandpa. It's a hot sunny day and a dog whines, but nobody takes much notice. Another dog walks by and hears the whining.

"What's the matter? Why are you whining?" asks the passing dog.
"I'm lying on a nail and it hurts," replies the first dog.
"Well why don't you do something about it?"
"It doesn't hurt enough."

How many whining dogs have you met, who talk about making a difference yet haven't got a strong enough reason why? I occasionally work with groups where it seems that most, if not all, are lying on some form of nail. At least now I can say, "Here, have a read of this book!"

15. Assess Your Motive For Action

Where there's no will, there's no way! When the reason is strong enough, you will do what is necessary. Strong willpower is always caused by a strong underlying purpose; a reason to put in the effort and take action. Reasons are the fuel behind the goal.

Without them, there will be no substantial progress. Strong reasons are what causes you to want the goal in the first place.

TIME TO WRITE

Focus on one of the areas you are considering making a difference about. Make a list of the reasons why you want to make this difference.

Go MAD about...

My reasons why are:
-
-
-
-
-
-
-

Now, on the next page, make a list of your reasons for not yet having made the difference. Include excuses you have previously made and any possible obstacles you identified.

My excuses and reasons for not making a difference:
-
-
-
-
-
-

"Dwell not upon thy weariness, thy strength shall be
according to the measure of thy desire."
Arabian Proverb

At this point, take the time to assess the two lists and make a
note of which reasons are the strongest.

16. Decide Which Direction You Are Moving In

Are you being pulled by a dream or pushed by circumstances? In
other words, when assessing your reasons why, do you notice that
you are tending to move towards gaining pleasure or moving away
from a specific source of pain? It doesn't matter which, but it is
important to know the difference. If you are seeking to move away
from the source of pain, your motive for continuing to take
further action is likely to diminish at some future point.

Let me give you an example relating to making a difference about
personal finances. Your strong reason why might be to avoid paying
interest on a credit card or to get rid of an overdraft. Both these
reasons are focused on moving away from something you don't

want. As the credit card bill and the overdraft reduce, the pain becomes less and might even become bearable. The danger is that the focus remains on the past e.g. "It's much better than it used to be," rather than refocusing and moving towards something you do want.

There is a strong link here with the second key principle of defining goals. Once you have defined meaningful goals, i.e. those linked with a strong reason why, you start heading in a direction. Without a direction, you will drift.

17. Identify What You Value

Whilst moving towards or away from things that give us pleasure or pain, we naturally move in line with our core values: those aspects of life we value as important. All goals and desires are vehicles for fulfilling our values. Hence, values influence the goals we choose and motivate us to take action. The stronger the values we hold, the greater our motive for action. If you don't have strongly held values, you will have little motivation.

Refer back to the previous activity where you listed the reasons why you wanted to make a specific difference. For each of those reasons answer the following question:

What makes this reason important to me?
-
-
-
-
-

This list will highlight some of the values you hold. Now ask yourself, "What makes these values important to me?" The answer to this question is likely to reveal a core value. If not, review the activity and consider if your reasons why are strong enough.

"Clarifying your values is the first step toward a richer, fuller, more productive life."
Carl Rogers

I sometimes give the following list of possible values to groups and ask them to identify those that are the most important to them.

Achievement	Family Happiness	Pleasure
Advancement	Freedom	Power
Adventure	Friendship	Recognition
Affection	Health	Responsibility
Competitiveness	Helpfulness	Self-respect
Co-operation	Inner Harmony	Spirituality
Creativity	Integrity	Wealth
Economic Security	Involvement	Wisdom
Fame	Loyalty	
	Personal Development	

Gaining greater insight into your core values will help you, later in the book, to develop goals that you consider worthwhile.

18. Don't Say It, If You Don't Mean It

I often smile to myself when people talk about their core values and then act differently, in accordance with their real values. You might fool yourself, but you will not fool any onlookers. Classic examples include people working 15 hours each day and stating their core values relate to family relationships, when they are often striving for economic security, recognition or achievement. Actions speak louder than words.

19. Make The Reason Why Stronger Than The Reason Not

"Good health and physical fitness are important." Most people would agree with this statement; but how important? Important enough to Go MAD about your own health and fitness? When people talk to me about losing weight or getting fitter, I now tend to ask, "What's your reason for wanting to?" Those that answer very often do not have a strong reason why, or lack conviction. There is frequently a strong link with their self-belief (principle four) which I will explain later.

Question: How does one become a butterfly?

Answer: You must want to fly so much, that you are willing to give up being a caterpillar.

When I consciously started to apply the Go MAD principles to my own health, I realised I needed a really strong reason why. So I linked it with one of my life ambitions – to live to a ripe old age. Looking around for role models, I realised that they tended not to be overweight. To put it bluntly, fat guys don't live as long! So my motivation – my strong *reason why* – is to live 10-20 years longer. If I've only got one life, I want to make the most of it. This, for me, is a compelling reason why I want to Go MAD about my health that is far stronger than all the reasons not to.

You must find your own reasons why. They must be important enough for you, not for someone else, if you really want to make a difference. An intensity of purpose – a burning desire – when harnessed to clear goals is a powerful source of energy. The more intense the feelings, the greater your motivation to Go MAD.

TIME TO WRITE

Consider your answers to the following questions:

What are you passionate about?

What is really, really important to you?

What makes you want to take action?

What would you like to be remembered for?

What makes life worth living?

20. Eliminate Trying

Have you ever asked someone to do something, or invited a person to go somewhere, and they have replied that they will *try* and do it, or *try* to attend? You know, and they know, that *try* really means, "I have not got a strong enough reason why, to definitely commit, but I don't want to upset you." Have you ever done that to someone else? Or even to yourself? Do you ever promise to yourself that you will *try* to do something?

Eliminate the word *try* from your language – unless you play rugby! In the majority of cases it serves no useful purpose; it programmes your mind with the possibility of not succeeding. Either plan to do it or decide not to. Be decisive. Notice the difference between saying, "I will *try* to make a difference," and, "I will make a difference." The latter has more resolve and indicates a stronger underlying reason why.

"Always bear in mind that your resolution to succeed is more important than any other factor."
Abraham Lincoln

If you are still not sure about the importance of eliminating this word, put your pen on the table. Now *try* to pick it up. Remember I asked you to *try* to pick it up, not to actually pick it up. It is pointless *trying*, and a waste of time. Develop a reason to successfully make a difference, or choose not to.

Watch out, or rather listen out, for people who are always *trying* to do things; *trying* to save money; *trying* to lose weight; or *trying* to complete a project on time. Notice also, the tone of voice that often accompanies *trying*. It is a good indicator that a strong motive for action is lacking, or the person lacks belief in their ability to achieve.

21. Move Beyond Thinking, "One day I will..."

Stop kidding yourself that you are going to do certain things, if you haven't had a strong enough reason to do them in the past. Has anything changed to strengthen your motivation? Well, something needs to, because unless it does, that day will never happen.

There is a big difference between pursuing a dream and following a fantasy. Dreams are attainable if you visualise in detail, start to plan a realistic way of accomplishing them and apply the seven key principles to make a difference. Fantasies are outside of your control. You have a better chance of being struck by lightning than winning the National Lottery.

Move beyond thinking, to positive action. If your reason why really is strong enough, define a goal and start to plan priorities. If you can't, or don't want to, then it is either a fantasy or you have not

40

got a strong enough reason why. Either do it or dump it; plan it or park it.

22.   Go MAD In Egypt (or not, as it happened)

I remember visiting Egypt and seeing the Sphinx in Cairo. The tour guide explained that the missing nose of the sphinx was in a museum in London. Caught up in holiday euphoria, my mind started to fantasise, "Wouldn't it be great to reunite the sphinx with its nose." I set a goal and started my plan of action. Several rolls of camera film were used and numerous postcards were purchased, all showing the noseless sphinx. I relaxed for the remainder of the holiday, knowing that I needed to continue my plan once I returned home.

Many years later and no further progress; the strength of my reason why, on a scale of one to ten, was one! I had discovered more important things to make a difference about.

Let me know if your core values relate to Egyptology and I will send you the photographs!

23.   Choose To Be Happy

Happiness is a choice. Choose to be happy rather than *trying* to be happy. Take personal responsibility (principle six) for being happy rather than blaming others and believing that they, or circumstances, are the cause of unhappiness. Remember the whining dog! More about this later in the book. For the moment, I just want you to challenge your thinking.

**"Every minute you are angry,
you lose sixty seconds of happiness."
Ralph Waldo Emerson**

TIME TO THINK

Do I think it is possible to decide certain emotions? (e.g. to be angry or unhappy.)

Do I believe it is possible to choose to be happy?

Do I take responsibility for doing this, or do I blame others?

24. If You Don't Enjoy It, Change Something

Whatever *it* is, when your heart is not in *it*, you don't enjoy *it*. You become less motivated by *it*, and less likely to make a difference about *it*. A strong reason why is lacking. So what are your options?

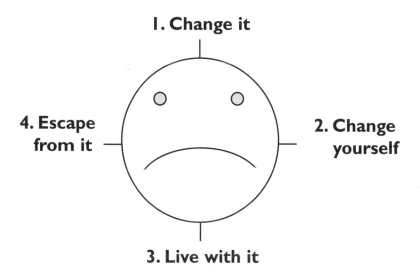

1. Change it

4. Escape from it

2. Change yourself

3. Live with it

Option 1 is not always possible. Sometimes *it* cannot be changed. Even if you can change *it*, you might not have a reason why that is strong enough to make a difference.

Option 2 is about changing the way you respond to *it*. You could focus on finding an enjoyable part of *it*. You could develop a more positive response to *it*. You could choose to appreciate the importance of *it*.

Option 3 is doing nothing about *it*. But, if you carry on doing *it*, stop whining about *it*. This might prove to be a difficult option if the nail becomes more painful!

Option 4 is finding another *it;* one that is enjoyable.

**"If I really want to improve my situation,
I can work on the one thing over which I have control –
myself."
Stephen R. Covey**

Let me give you a personal example. In 1985, I was working very long hours for a major bank. My role involved lending money, which I was good at – but did not particularly enjoy. The large amount of paperwork that I had to complete often appeared never-ending. I found myself disliking the job more and more. Something needed to change.

I attempted to change the way the job was done (option 1) but spent much wasted energy banging my head against a brick wall – the bank's procedures. Several managers made comments like, "If you want to become a manager, you have to endure what we went through. We know what it's like to work long hours!" I abandoned option 1 and moved straight to option 3. At the time I did not believe it was possible to change my feelings towards the role or the organisation. Option 2, therefore, was not a viable option. For over six months I attempted to live with the situation (option 3) but not without whining! I became envious of my friends who appeared to enjoy their jobs and eventually the nail became so painful I chose option 4. I left the bank for a more enjoyable job and the start of a new career in training and development.

If I had known then what I know now, it would have taken me much less than the eleven months it did take to make a difference! If you don't enjoy something, choose which option to take. The decision is your responsibility (principle six). Have you got a strong enough reason why you want to make a difference?

25. Escape From The Rut

Discomfort can become unnoticeable over a period of time and may even be accepted as the norm. The effort of doing something about it can be perceived as more uncomfortable than the current discomfort. For many people, avoiding embarrassment or failure can be a stronger reason why not to attempt something, than the potential outcome or desired results. Hence, nothing happens.

Why do so many people, who are unhappy at work, wait until

their jobs are made redundant before moving to one that they enjoy more? Because it doesn't hurt enough, yet. A comfortable rut can be a dangerous rut. Mark McCormack, in *What they don't teach you at Harvard Business School* makes the following link between aligning your work with your values:

"If you're bored it's your fault. You just aren't working hard enough at making your job interesting. It is also probably the reason you haven't been offered anything better. Find out what you love to do and you will be successful at it."

Have you heard the expression: "Get a life"? I have heard it used sarcastically and out of desperation or exasperation. In order to escape from the rut, you need a reason why. So let's be more focused:

Get a life ……………….. get a reason why!

---

26. Remind Yourself With A Trigger

Various things can act as an internal reminder of the strength of your reason why. These *triggers* could be:

- a key word that you say to yourself.
- a statement or phrase (e.g. written on a bookmark or computer screensaver).
- a picture of something.
- a visual image in your mind.
- a deliberate physical action you make (e.g. a way of clenching your hand).

It could be a combination of these things. Many successful sports players deliberately create and use internal reminders to help them achieve success. If you have ever watched tennis at Wimbledon, you might have noticed many of the players giving themselves internal reminders between games or before important points in matches.

TIME TO THINK

What is the thing (or combination of things) that would act as the trigger to prompt you to take further action?

Ensure that your trigger is as powerful and strong as it can possibly be. Test it a few times. Remember that the trigger is only useful if the reason why is strong enough in the first place. Make sure you are not left with 50 postcards of a noseless sphinx!

TIME TO REFLECT

Having reached the end of this section, consider the following questions. You might find it useful to discuss your answers with someone you trust.

What has prevented me in the past from making a difference?

What have been some of my most powerful reasons why that have resulted in action?

What are my core values?

What ruts do I want to escape from?

What dreams do I want to pursue?

What have I learned about Go MAD Principle One?

What are the implications?

What practical steps could I take to develop a stronger reason why?

"**We think too small.
Like the frog at the bottom of the well.
He thinks the sky is only as big
as the top of the well.
If he surfaced, he would have
an entirely different view.**"
Mao Tse-Tung

Principle Two

DEFINE YOUR GOAL

BEFORE STARTING TO

GO MAD

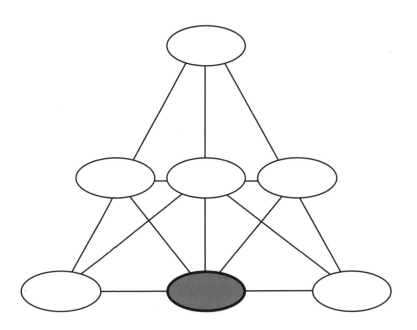

"Those who really seek the path to
enlightenment dictate terms to their mind.
They then proceed with strong determination."
Buddha

27.   Decide To Be More Than Average

The average person does not have well-defined personal goals. It is commonly stated, in many books, that only 3-5% of the population have written goals. By the end of this section you will have an understanding of goal defining techniques. If you apply these techniques with the other key principles, you could seriously affect your success in a positive way. Remember you will never achieve more than you set out to achieve. **Most people aim at nothing and hit it with incredible accuracy**. Your ability to learn and regularly apply the skills of goal defining will have a major influence on determining your future.

"If you can't accurately define what you want, how will you know when you've achieved the difference?"
Andy Gilbert

---

28.   Understand Your Natural Ability

I realise that, for some people, the word *goals* can be a turnoff. You don't have to use this word! During our research many people referred to: *targets, specific objectives, well-formed outcomes, having an end in mind,* the *destination* or simply *knowing what they wanted.* Many referred to it as "the thing I wanted to achieve". To survive in life, you have developed goal-orientated habits. If you have ever travelled on holiday or set out for a destination, you have experienced moving towards a goal.

"I'm not goal orientated!" stated someone on a recent development programme, "I like to go on holiday and do nothing – just to drift around and enjoy life." I resisted the temptation of asking him how he had managed to attend the course on time, without having a goal of doing so. Instead, I helped him to realise that each year he successfully achieved his goal of deliberately being in an environment and creating a state of mind that allowed him to relax and do what he wanted. He had, in fact, made a difference from being in his normal pressurised working environment and, without realising it, successfully applied all seven Go MAD key principles.

"It concerns us to know the purpose we seek in life, for then... we shall be more likely to attain what we want."
Aristotle

---

29. Define Your Own Success

What is the meaning of success? The answer to this question depends upon the meaning *you* give to it. Earlier, I asked you to write your definition of success. Refer back to it and check what you have written.

When I use this exercise with groups, the two words most commonly used in definitions (by 60-70% of people) are *achievement* and *goals*. I find this somewhat ironic, bearing in mind the much smaller percentage who make the effort to define written personal goals. Maybe this is why so many individuals do not consider themselves to be successful!

My favourite definition is the one given by Earl Nightingale who spent over 30 years researching and broadcasting success principles:

"Success is the progressive realisation of a worthwhile goal, or the pursuit of a worthy ideal."

You determine what *you* consider to be worthwhile or a worthy ideal, depending on *your* core values and the strength of *your* reason why.

"To laugh often and much; to win the respect of intelligent people and the affection of children; to earn the appreciation of honest critics and endure the betrayal of false friends; to appreciate beauty; to find the best in others; to leave the world a bit better whether by a healthy child, a garden patch, or a redeemed social condition; to know even one life has breathed easier because you have lived.
This is to have succeeded."
Ralph Waldo Emerson

Last year I was talking with John, aged 33, whose core values are based upon economic security for himself and his family. He was totally focused on the goal of reaching the age of 50, so he could retire financially secure. Successfully pursuing a career in the banking and finance sector, John had great self-belief in his own abilities and the achievability of his goal; had involved others in the detailed planning of his financial and career priorities, and was taking responsibility for making it happen.

30. Link Success With Personal Happiness

Achieving the goal or attaining the end result is a measure of success; unfortunately it is often mistaken for the only measure. The journey towards the end goal might contain several sub-goals and milestones of achievement. If success is the progressive realisation of a worthwhile goal, why not seek to enjoy the journey as well as the destination?

"Happiness is a state of mind where your thoughts are pleasant for the greater share of the time."
Maxwell Maltz

For some, the end result is all that matters; for others, the process of getting there is equally, if not more, important. I regularly come across individuals who are looking forward to their retirement date from work. I often hear them discussing what they will do: "When I retire in… years time." Incredibly this end goal of retirement varies from a few months to over twenty years! If happiness is a measure of success, how successful will they have been in the progressive realisation of their goal?

"To seek personal fulfilment only outside of work and to ignore the significant portion of our lives we spend working would be to limit our opportunities to be happy and complete human beings."
Peter Senge

Doing what you enjoy and consider to be worthwhile, will increase your happiness. Deciding what you want and working towards your goals are steps towards meeting the personal success criteria you have defined.

31. Decide What You Want

Goals direct your actions; your actions create results. Without goals there is no direction, resulting in a lack of focused action.

Imagine a ship setting out to sail without determining a destination or direction. There would be no progress; it would drift out to sea, bumping into obstacles as it bobbed around. Think about people that you know who are perhaps in a similar situation!

Occasionally I get asked, "How can I decide goals when I don't know what I want?" I have discovered four main methods of successfully doing this:

1. *Imagine* that you do know what you want.
2. Go back to principle one and examine your core values and strength of reason why.
3. Decide a specific time by which you will have decided what you want, i.e. set a goal about defining another goal.
4. Explore your hopes and dreams: consider your ruts and circumstances.

"I'll tell you what I want. What I really, really want."
The Spice Girls

---

32.   Focus On The What

If you want to make a difference, focus on defining your desired outcome. What do you want to have, do or become?

TIME TO THINK

Consider the areas you want to Go MAD about.

What do you want to have or acquire? (material goals)

What do you want to do or achieve? (activity goals)

What do you want to become? (developmental goals)

Whilst the first two types of goal are relatively straightforward to understand, the third requires further explanation. It includes goals relating to developing skills and knowledge, gaining experience, improving personal behaviour or relationships, and increasing effectiveness. In order to achieve your material and activity goals it might be necessary first to develop yourself.

"Work to become, not to acquire."
Elbert Hubbard

TIME TO REFLECT

If your goals are all material goals, ask yourself the following two questions:

What are the personal characteristics possessed by others, who have successfully achieved these goals?

In order to achieve these goals, how do I need to develop?

---

33.   Leave The How For Later

You should be careful of the "Yes, but how?" syndrome. This is a common and deadly disease that all too often kills goals before they are fully defined. For example:

I want to develop new skills.
Yes, but how do I make the time?
I want to increase my income.
Yes, but how?

I want to...
Yes, but how is someone like me going to achieve that?

The "Yes, but how?" syndrome can be contagious. It is quite quickly spread from the mouth of one person to the ears of another. If it is not immediately diagnosed, it will kill an idea before a strong enough reason why can be found and a goal defined. Worse still, the syndrome can remain with you and become a habit unless treated by applying Go MAD key principle four.

Obstacles are those frightening things you see when you take your eyes off the goal.

Focusing on *how* to make a difference before fully defining exactly *what* the difference is, causes most people to give up before really starting. "There's no point in setting a goal, because I can't see how to get there." If only life was that easy and predictable! Focus on the why and the what (principles one and two) and leave the how (principles three to seven) for later.

34. Recognise The Givens

It is important to consider the price you are prepared to pay in achieving your goal. What are you willing to do more of? What are you willing to stop doing or do less of? The answers to these questions should give you an indication of the strength of your reason why. With this in mind, consider the extent to which you believe you can realistically control or directly influence the desired outcome.

Go MAD – the art of making a difference

Focus your energy on the things you can influence and make a difference about. Recognise that some things exist that cannot be changed. It's pointless moaning about the weather or being stuck in a traffic jam – they are both *givens*. You can't change either of them, but you can make a difference by choosing how to respond to the givens.

"Give us the grace to accept with serenity the things that cannot be changed, courage to change the things that can be changed, and the wisdom to distinguish the one from the other."
Reinhold Niebuhr

In any organisation, there will always be certain rules and procedures. Some of these can probably be improved for the benefit of all; others will be givens. Examples might include: Government and European legislation, working terms and conditions, legal contracts, and safety procedures. In seeking to Go MAD accept what you cannot change and change what you cannot accept.

TIME TO WRITE

Focus on the area or issue you want to Go MAD about, to identify what you can influence and which aspects are givens.

What can I influence?	What are the givens?
-	-
-	-
-	-
-	-
-	-

35. Develop Your Goal Writing Ability

Yes, it is important to have your goals written down. Research has shown that people with written defined goals achieve substantially greater results than those who don't. Writing goals down is evidence of a serious intent to Go MAD. It starts the process of moving an idea in the mind, from your imagination to the external reality.

A well-written goal gives precision and clarity of direction. There are some important steps in writing goals that need to be taken. First, you must develop the ability to turn a vague aim into a specific, measurable goal.

When I left school, I thought I wanted to be a bank manager – so I went to work in a bank. My career aim was to be a young manager of a large high street branch. If at the time you had asked me about my short-term goals, I would probably have mentioned passing the banking exams, gaining more experience and being promoted to the next grade. However, with hindsight I realise that these were aims and not goals. So, what is the difference?

1.   Goals are *specific* in their detail; whereas aims are vague. In my example I was not specific about the age I was aiming to be a manager by or exactly how large the high street branch would be. I was also unclear about what experience I wanted to gain.

2.   Goals are *measurable* in either time, cost, quantity or quality; whereas aims cannot be measured. In my examples I included two possible measures: passing exams and gaining promotion. However, I did not specify by what date these events would happen.

A goal is a dream with a deadline.

---

3. You have to believe that the goal is *achievable* within the timescale you decide. For a goal to be achievable, you must believe there is at least a 50% probability of success. This link with self-belief (principle four) is referred to in a later section.

4. Goals should be *relevant and related* to a strong underlying reason why. Aims often tend to be more wishful thinking.

5. Goals have *timescales* to measure what will be achieved by a certain date. Aims often have vague timescales or none at all.

There are many books that refer to goal defining and most use the acronym SMART to describe best practice.

Specific
Measurable
Achievable
Relevant
Timescales

Knowing what SMART means and having the ability to write SMART goals are two different things. Most of the managers who attend Go MAD development programmes have heard of SMART goals and can recite what each letter stands for. However, I estimate that less than 20% can actually write a SMART goal in a single sentence.

TIME TO WRITE

It is now your opportunity to write a SMART goal in a single sentence. Choose something relevant with a strong reason why; that you believe is achievable within a certain timescale, and state specifically the measurable difference you want to make.

My SMART goal (first draft)

In the following few sections, you will discover extra tips and ideas about refining and amending your goal to increase your probability of success.

36. Be More Specific

Defined goals focus only on the *what*. Remember to leave the *how* for later – there is no need to include it in a written goal.

Amend and clarify any of the following words you have included in your written goal:

improved	-	specify a measurable improvement
better	-	specify how much better
more	-	specify how much more
less	-	specify how much less
feel	-	specify what you will feel
wish	-	state what *will* happen

TIME TO THINK

A good check of how specific your goal is, is to notice which of your five senses you will be using to measure your success. What will you be able to see, hear, feel/touch, taste or smell by your specified date that is a measurable difference? If you had to audit yourself on a specific date in the future, what would be the tangible evidence of success?

During a recent Go MAD development session, I asked the previous questions to the participants to help them define their goals. One of them, Anthea, had written the following SMART goal: *"To have my graduation picture on my mantelpiece by 31ˢᵗ July."* This is a great example of a measurable goal with a timescale; a goal that is simple, yet specifically written. I asked Anthea how achievable she believed this to be and she stated that she had already bought the picture frame!

37. Understand The Purpose Of Your Subconscious Mind

I am about to explain to you in simple terms, how a part of your mind can be programmed to automatically ensure your goals are successfully achieved. Most people go their whole lives without knowing how to use the greatest success mechanism at their immediate disposal. By understanding and developing your ability to apply this information, you will dramatically increase your ability to make a difference. **I recommend that you review the following ten pages a few times, before continuing with the rest of the book.**

"For one who has conquered the mind,
the mind is the best of friends,
but for one who has failed to do so,
his mind will be the greatest enemy."
Bhagavad-Gita

You have two minds; your conscious mind and your subconscious mind. The conscious mind is the one you use to think with. Its functions include: decision making, logic, forming judgements and deliberate thinking. However, the conscious mind cannot cope with being aware of everything going on (most people can focus on only 5-9 things happening at the same time) so the majority of information is filtered into the subconscious mind.

Your subconscious mind stores all information it receives from sight, sound, touch, taste and smell. It also records everything you do, including your words, thoughts, actions and feelings. All this information is stored in your memory, even if sometimes it appears that your conscious mind cannot remember something.

The working of your conscious mind is influenced by the subconscious mind and the information stored in it. For example, if you have had lots of negative thoughts about a situation, and feel unhappy about it, these will have been stored away and are likely to influence your conscious decisions in the future.

**"Your results are influenced by what you
think about most of the time.
So keep focused on what you want,
instead of what you don't want."
Andy Gilbert**

Your subconscious mind automatically responds to instructions given to it by your conscious mind, it cannot act on its own initiative. It has to be given goals to achieve, or problems to solve, before it can function. Hence, no goals – no functioning. The goals increase the alertness of your mind so that you become consciously aware of information that is relevant to what you want. This information might already be stored in your memory. If it isn't, your subconscious mind will heighten the awareness of your conscious mind to find it. Hence, the purpose of the subconscious mind is to achieve the goals and problems you define.

38.   Programme Your Mind With Goals And Instructions

Let me give you a couple of everyday examples to help you understand this important process.

One evening, about six weeks ago, I lost my shaver. I don't know how I lost it; I just did. I looked in all the obvious places where it might normally be, but I couldn't find it. I analysed where I might have put it, retraced my movements of the last few hours, and looked in all the obvious places once more – still no success. After approximately 20 minutes of fruitless searching, I remembered that I had only used the logical and analytical thinking of my conscious mind. The information I needed was stored in my subconscious mind. At some stage earlier I had been holding my shaver, carried it somewhere, put it down, and seen where I had left it. All this information had been stored in my subconscious mind, I just needed to access it.

I set the following SMART goal: *To locate the shaver before I went to bed,* and repeated it to myself. I relaxed, believing that my subconscious mind would start searching for the information. I cannot recall what I did for the next three hours or so, until I decided to go to bed. By this time I had actually forgotten about the goal. As I sat on my bed, I had a thought, "The shaver is in the spare bedroom next to my sports bag." Sure enough, it was!

"They can, because they think they can."
Virgil

I use this technique whenever I temporarily forget something. Most often, this is when I'm talking to someone and want to recall the name of a book, a person or a piece of music. Many people might say something like, "I can't remember the name," or "I've forgotten what it was called." This is because they are using their conscious mind in an attempt to recall the information. Next time this happens to you consciously programme your subconscious mind with a specific goal. For example, I commonly say, "I'll remember the name within the next 30 seconds," or "By the time we've finished speaking, I'll have remembered that piece of information." It works – but only if you relax and believe it will work!

Have you ever misplaced a set of keys, a pen or something and struggled to find the missing item? Have you ever said things like, "I'll never find it," or, "I give up"? Well if you have, these words or thoughts will be stored automatically in your subconscious mind, which will not be activated to help you. Not only that, but your conscious mind will also be affected and you will either continue your search in the same way, or give up.

"Your subconscious mind is like a powerful internet search engine, capable of accessing the websites of your life experiences."
Andy Gilbert

Like a computer, your subconscious mind has to be programmed with instructions in order to function effectively. If you don't give it precise instructions it cannot give you the solutions you desire. The more detailed and specific the instructions, the more detailed and specific the results; put garbage in and you will get garbage out. This is important to remember, because your subconscious mind cannot consciously think. It cannot question the instructions it receives and it is therefore crucial to ensure they are positive.

39. Eliminate Worry

If you are using your conscious mind to worry about things, or to think strongly about failure, recognise that you are negatively programming your subconscious mind to bring them into reality. This is because it cannot tell the difference between negative and positive instructions. Focusing on what you don't want to happen is a form of negative goal setting. Your results will be determined by your dominant thoughts, whether they be positive goals or negative fears; you get what you focus on.

Imagine playing a sport involving hand and eye co-ordination, and worrying about what you don't want to happen. If you focus on what might go wrong, you are more likely to get it.

In golf, if you focus on where you don't want the ball to go (e.g. the bunker) you will be less effective than if you focus on where you do want the ball to go.

"Why look for the worst in people when you can look for the great in them. Whatever you look for, you will find."
Andy Gilbert

---

40. Filter Out Negative Thoughts

Because the subconscious mind also stores all the information you receive from your five senses, it can be easily influenced by the negative suggestions of other people – if you allow their words to dwell in your conscious mind. Increase your awareness of how you react to the comments of others. Take care about accepting criticism as reality. Differentiate between useful feedback, that enables you to develop, and destructive negative comments. By consciously filtering out the negatives, you prevent them being stored by the subconscious mind.

"I will not allow anyone to walk through my mind with their dirty feet."
Mahatma Gandhi

Every time you consciously think of something it gets recorded in your subconscious mind. Not surprisingly, if you keep thinking the same thought on a frequent basis, you will strengthen the memory of it. Criticisms and negative comments that you have repeatedly heard from other people, can after a period of time be imprinted so deeply in your subconscious mind that they become limiting beliefs, which further strengthens them. It is your responsibility for consciously controlling your thoughts by choosing what to accept from others and focusing positively on what you want.

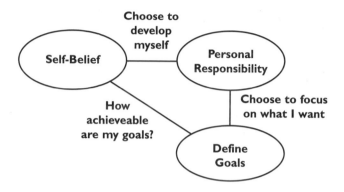

Later in the book you will discover ways to increase your self-belief which will enable you to maintain momentum towards achieving your defined goals.

41. Develop Clarity

It is important for goals to have clarity. The clearer the goal, the easier it is for the subconscious mind to either recall or generate awareness of information that will be helpful in making a difference. You might have experienced this when shopping for a specific item. If you know exactly what you want, you will become aware of where to find it.

Imagine taking a photograph with a manual camera. You will need to adjust the focus of the lens. If you don't have a clear, sharp image of the subject, you will not get the results you desire.

Remember the previous example of Anthea's goal: sharply focused on her graduation photograph; so detailed that she could describe the photo frame and its position on her mantelpiece.

42. Use Your Imagination

Walt Disney died before Disney World in Florida opened. A reporter, interviewing his brother Roy, commented that it was, "Unfortunate that Walt did not live to see it built." Quick as a flash his brother replied, "Walt *saw* it first. That's why you're seeing it now."

Imagine the detail of Walt Disney's vision of the future. What an inspirational role model to have.

"You've got to have a dream.
If you don't have a dream
How you gonna have a dream come true?"
Richard Rogers and Oscar Hammerstein

The desire to succeed is often demonstrated by world-class athletes. Sally Gunnell, having achieved World Championship and Olympic success, commented on the link between self-belief and visualised goals:

"If I visualise success then I will be able to achieve it."

Linford Christie, after winning his Gold medal in the 100 metres at the Barcelona Olympics, stated:

"They said I was too old, but I did it. I had practised in my mind and saw myself do it."

Visualising your future success is a way of strengthening the link between the first two Go MAD principles. If your vision is stronger than your current reality, you will move in that direction; if the current reality is stronger, you will stay where you are. Because your subconscious mind does not consciously think, it cannot differentiate between reality and imagined experiences; it just stores data that goes through your conscious mind. So, the more vividly you can imagine succeeding, the better. You will reap the rewards of the positive thoughts you sow in your own mind.

"Whatever the mind can conceive and believe, it can achieve."
Napoleon Hill

If you visualise success and programme your mind with well-defined goals, your subconscious mind will act as a success mechanism. Whilst there is a need to recognise challenges and anticipate possible obstacles, the focus must be on facing and overcoming them. If you programme your mind with fear and negative thinking, your subconscious mind will act as a failure mechanism.

I am fascinated by how the mind works, so in 2005 I wrote a book entitled "Brain Magic" with Nancy Slessenger – a brain researcher who makes the science stuff easy to understand. Together we researched the 100 most common questions, people wanted to know the answers to, about the brain and the way we think. If you are interested in discovering more about programming your mind and the way you think, then visit www.brainmagic.co.uk. You don't have to even buy the actual book as you can download an e-book for a fraction of the cost of the paperback. It contains lots of fascinating facts, tips and techniques to help you make a difference and live a longer, happier and healthier life.

TIME TO THINK

Focus on a specific date in the future within the next five years. Imagine that you have travelled forward in time to meet yourself as you will be in the future having achieved the goals you want to achieve. Imagine seeing yourself, perhaps even shaking hands with this future person.

What do you see?

What is this person doing?

What is this person like?

What does this person look like?

What are the differences you notice?

What have they done with their life during the past few months or years?

Repeat or adapt this exercise, linking it with a strong reason why and a defined goal. One way of doing this is to involve a friend to read the questions as you sit relaxed, with your eyes closed. Use your imagination and develop the clarity of your vision.

Make your future vision irresistible by intensifying some of the elements:

- Add movement to turn a still picture into a moving picture.
- Make the images three-dimensional.
- Increase the size and brightness of your images.
- Add vivid colours.
- Develop a musical soundtrack to accompany the images.
- Increase the volume and experiment with an exciting upbeat tempo.
- Hear the sounds of encouragement.
- See it through your own eyes as if you are actually experiencing this future success.
- Enjoy it and notice your feelings of attraction towards the goal.
- Intensify your feelings.
- Build in your trigger reminder (from section 26).

If you have continued reading without doing this exercise, you will not appreciate the significance of it. That's your loss. Why not have a go, with a difference you want to make, and notice what happens? I work on the basis that if it is effective for Walt Disney, top athletes and others who successfully make a difference, it can be effective for anyone else who *really* wants to Go MAD for themselves.

"All men dream; but not equally.
Those who dream at night in the
dusty recesses of their minds wake
in the day to find that it was vanity:
but the dreamers of the day are dangerous men,
for they may act their dreams
with open eyes, to make it possible."
T.E. Lawrence

---

43. Decide On Your Own Success Criteria

Avoid comparative goals. Goals that include comparisons, relinquish control over the outcome by being dependent upon the performance of others. Top class athletes all monitor their personal best performances and seek to improve them against the success criteria they determine as benchmarks.

I have worked with several organisations where *being the best* had an adverse effect on both the morale of staff and performance of the business. With the competitive nature of being the best, only one individual or team can achieve the goal. Striving to do this can lead to people withholding information and not sharing examples of best practice with colleagues. On several occasions, I have witnessed individuals achieving their goals at the expense of team performance, and teams achieving their goals to the detriment of company performance. Often this is done in order to gain recognition from others.

**"Too many people spend money they haven't earned,
to buy things they don't want,
to impress people they don't like."
Will Rogers**

Imagine an exam where you set the pass mark. If you set it too high, you might not believe it is possible to achieve; if you set it too low, you will not gain a sense of achievement. You must set the success criteria of your goal according to what you consider to be worthwhile.

**"If it's too easy, you won't care to do it.
If it's too hard, you won't dare to do it."
Andy Gilbert**

44. Develop Sub-goals And Form Success Habits

Sometimes the difference you want to make may need breaking down into a series of steps or sub-goals. This might be because of the size of the goal or the timescale involved. For larger goals it is important to have sub-goals for several reasons:

- To measure progress.
- To feel successful in moving towards the desired outcome.
- To increase self-belief about achieving the end goal.

**Question: How do you eat an elephant?
Answer: One bite at a time.**

Each time a sub-goal is reached, it is important to acknowledge your success and congratulate yourself. You can develop the habit of *winning* by simply saying to yourself, "That's a win!" after each sub-goal you achieve. This causes your success to be recorded by your subconscious mind. Frequent small successes cause a regular pattern of success to be stored in your subconscious mind. Once a successful procedure has been established it will develop into a subconscious habit. For example, riding a bike, driving a car and playing a sport. In other words, you don't have to consciously think about every aspect of what you do.

David Beckham in striking a football does not consciously think about the precise angle, direction and spin of the ball. His subconscious mind is aware of the goal. He focuses on the ball and allows his subconscious to perform the action, knowing that it has been successfully performed many times before.

TIME TO WRITE

Revisit the goal you defined earlier and decide if it would be helpful to develop small sub-goals. If so write them in the box below, ensuring that each sub-goal is also SMART.

What will be achieved?	By what date?

This is a great exercise to undertake if you want to Go MAD about your weight or fitness. Whilst writing this book, I set myself this challenge and during 3 months lost 20lbs to achieve my target weight, whilst increasing my fitness to the highest it had been for 10 years. I had monthly and weekly sub-goals relating to achieving my target weights and visits to the gym. Doing it this way meant I only had to reduce my weight by one or two pounds each week and visit the gym every two or three days. This was very achievable in my own mind. Focusing on achieving sub-goals made a big difference from focusing on fifteen hours of fitness and aerobic training each month and seeking to lose twenty pounds of fat!

A quick word of advice if you are thinking of making a difference about your health or fitness: avoid defining goals about weight loss. Instead, define your desired goal and sub-goal weight. Remember, focus on what you want to become, not what you want to lose.

45. Seek Harmony Between Your Goals

Check that your goals do not conflict with each other. If they do, for whatever reason, do something about it. Common conflicts include:

- Too many goals and not enough time.
- Personal goals conflict with work goals.
- Goals do not include partner's involvement.
- Goals are not aligned with core values.
- Achieving one goal would mean not achieving another goal.
- Conflict with the goals of others who are important.
- The achievement of goals would adversely affect others.

TIME TO REFLECT

If you have already developed several well-defined goals, check to ensure there is harmony between them.

46. Get Used To Goal Defining

Sometimes I get asked about the most effective timescales for goals. This is different for different people and depends greatly upon the strength of your reason why. What one person describes as short-term, might be viewed as long-term by someone else.

Having done many goal defining exercises with individuals and groups, I have included several to help you get used to thinking about and writing your goals.

**"You can't achieve a goal that isn't there,
or a target which cannot be seen."
Andy Gilbert**

TIME TO WRITE

Let's start with short-term goals:

What do you believe you will achieve that is worthwhile by the end of today?

What do you believe you will achieve that is worthwhile by the end of the week?

What do you believe you will achieve that is worthwhile by the end of the month?

What do you believe you will achieve that is worthwhile by this time next year?

47. Have Daily Goals

Get into the habit of being successful by achieving something worthwhile each day. Make a small difference daily. Write a simple SMART goal at the start of each day that you believe you will achieve.

48. Go MAD In A Year

What do you want to achieve in the next twelve months that you believe is possible? Make a list of eight specific goals. Because you can imagine the year ahead, and foresee certain events that you know will happen, your goals are likely to be achieved. Only write down those goals that relate to what you really want to have, do or become.

TIME TO WRITE

Eight goals I want to achieve during the next year:

1.

2.

3.

4.

5.

6.

7.

8.

If you are in a serious relationship, consider doing this as a joint exercise with your partner. I encouraged my parents to do this exercise and they ended up buying a new caravan! This was as a direct result of them considering joint retirement goals of places to visit.

49.   Read And Review Your Written Goals

Keep your goals visible and ensure you review them on a regular basis. This will remind your conscious mind and imprint them more deeply on your subconscious mind. I have met some individuals who even write their goals out on a daily basis, just for this purpose. It only takes a few minutes and certainly works for them.

I keep my goals in my daily planner, with reminders to review and amend them on a monthly and quarterly basis. Find a place that works for you. A friend of mine has stuck a copy of his main goal in the centre of his car steering wheel.

Remember that most people don't have written goals or understand the importance of them. Only share your personal goals with people who have goals of their own, understand the importance of yours, and that you choose to involve.

**"People who say that life is not worthwhile
are really saying that they themselves
have no personal goals which are worthwhile."
Maxwell Maltz**

---

50.   Know When To Extend Or Amend Your Goal

There are several reasons to extend or amend your goal:

*   If you notice that your reason why is not strong enough to sustain your continued effort. It might be that you consider

another goal more worthwhile. Stop pursuing an existing goal if you consider it no longer worthwhile.

- If you realise at a later stage that your goal is not SMART enough. You might need to be more specific about the measurable outcome or timescale.

- If your self-belief drops and the probability of achieving the outcome within the timescale falls below 50%.

- When you approach completion. It is often necessary at this point to define new goals as there is a common tendency for many people to slow down if no further goals exist.

For more information about advanced goal defining techniques, helping others to define goals and example case-studies, please refer to the book "Go MAD about Coaching." It includes an audio CD with examples of me helping a person define different types of goals and using the Go MAD Framework to help their thinking.

TIME TO REFLECT

Having reached the end of this section, consider the following questions:

What do I want to Go MAD about?

How will I know when I've achieved my goal?

How will I know that I'm making progress?

What effect will this outcome have on others and myself?

Is having this outcome worth the effort it will take to achieve it?

What is important about achieving this outcome?

What have I discovered about the way my mind works?

What have I learned about Go MAD Principle Two?

What are the implications?

What actions do I want to consider?

"Fatigue is often caused not by work,
but by worry, frustration and resentment.
We rarely get tired when we are
doing something interesting and exciting."
Dale Carnegie

Principle Three

PLAN YOUR PRIORITIES

BEFORE TAKING ACTION

TO

GO MAD

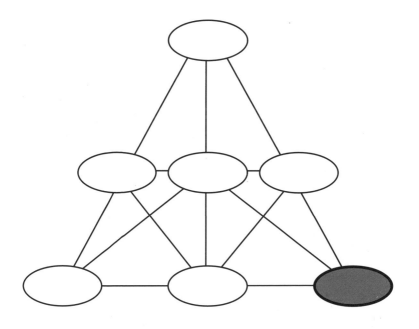

"If you don't stand for something,
you'll fall for anything.
But if your goals are vivid,
specific, flexible and supported
by action plans and sub-goals,
you'll believe that your life is worth living.
And you'll be right."
Denis Waitley

51. Use The Three Letter Word

Now that you have a reason why and defined what you want, the time has come to consider *how* it can be done. This three letter word often separates those who will Go MAD from those who won't.

Those who fail to Go MAD ask, "Can I do it?" and are guided by impossibility.

Those who succeed ask, "*How* can I do it?" and devise a strategy based upon evaluating possibilities. They have self-belief that they can do it and just need to discover how.

52. Prepare For The Journey

You have identified your destination and know why you want to go there. Now you need to prepare for the journey and plan your priorities before taking action. Time spent planning will be saved many times over as you progress towards achieving your goal.

"The future belongs to those who prepare for it."
Ralph Waldo Emerson

You have already broken your larger goal into smaller sub-goals. Now you need to identify possible actions that will take you towards achieving each of your sub-goals. In the following sections you will discover:

- How to make the best use of your time.
- The importance of exploring ten possibility thinking areas.
- How to prioritise the most important ideas.
- Methods of planning time.
- Ways of working smarter instead of harder.

I recognise that the thought of planning and preparation can be a turn off for some people. It is for me on occasions. If this happens, use your personal motivational trigger (section 26) to remind yourself of your strong reason why.

53. Control Self Instead Of Managing Time

There is no such thing as time management. Time cannot be controlled or managed; it just passes. The only thing you can control is yourself and how you use your time.

At the start of each week, you are given 168 hours. Each day you receive 1440 minutes. Each 8-hour working day you have 28,800 seconds. At the end of a working day, you have an amount of time at your disposal. You choose what to do with that time.

**"What you choose to do with your time,
will determine your future results."
Andy Gilbert**

Everyone has the same amount of time. You cannot save time; you can only spend it. Time spent doing one thing cannot be spent on another. You have to prioritise and make choices; it is totally your responsibility.

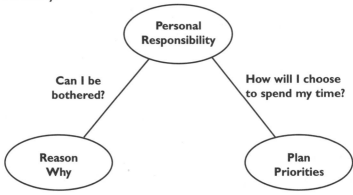

84

How often have you heard the comment, "But I haven't got time!" Translating this phrase into Go MAD language, it really means, "I choose not to make time available, because I don't consider this activity important enough and haven't got a strong enough reason why."

Making a difference involves choosing how you spend your time, prioritising which activities need more or less time and allocating future time to achieving those goals you consider to be worthwhile.

54. Generate Lots Of Possibilities

The key word to emphasise is *possibilities*. It might be too early to decide definite actions, so keep thinking about possibilities, ideas and alternatives.

TIME TO WRITE

I suggest you use a separate piece of paper to write your lists. When doing this activity, aim to generate quantity. Remember they are only possibilities – you can evaluate and prioritise later.

1. **What possible tasks or things could help you in achieving your goal? Include all the ideas you have.**

2. **What possible resources might be useful?**

3. **What possible reasons are there to involve others? How could they help?**

4. **Who could possibly help you?**

5. **How could you communicate your goal to them? Cont...**

6. **How could you possibly obtain their help and get them committed to helping you?**

7. **What possible obstacles might you encounter?**

8. **What possible risks or implications might there be in pursuing your goal?**

9. **How could you possibly overcome those obstacles and minimise any risks?**

10. **What assumptions might you be making? What might you be taking for granted?**

Setting aside time to do possibility thinking about these ten areas is a key element in using Go MAD as a thinking system. It will cause you to think deeper and wider if you explore possibilities before making a decision. When I coach individuals using Go MAD to help their thinking I often look to generate 50-100 possibilities; when working with teams on business improvement projects we commonly generate 300-1000 ideas.

"Don't skim the surface if you want to catch the big fish."
Andy Gilbert

Firstly think possibilities; secondly decide priorities; and thirdly plan time in your diary to do the priorities. These are the three elements of the third Go MAD key principle.

55. Differentiate Between Urgent And Important

To maximise the use of your time, it is essential to understand the difference between actions that are important and those that are urgent. Some actions might be both important and urgent, and some might be neither. Differentiating between urgent and important actions is necessary in considering what needs to be done first.

Important actions are those you identify as being critical to the achievement of your goal. *Urgent* actions are those that demand immediate attention.

TIME TO THINK

Review your list and decide whether each possible action is: urgent; important; both urgent and important, or neither.

56. Decide The Elements Of Your Action Plan

There are many different formats for action plans – many of which are over complicated. However, the basis of any personal action plan is the same:

What will I do? (actions)	By when? (date)

A copy of this basic form of action plan is included in section 129 of this book for you to use. A copy of the more detailed action plan I used to achieve my health and fitness goal is also included. You might want to remind yourself of your SMART goal, or have a list of your sub-goals on your action plan; that is for you to decide. Other common elements of action plans include start and finish dates, who else will be involved, review dates, success measurement criteria and rewards.

The key to a good action plan is designing one for yourself that you feel happy using. Avoid falling into the common traps of making it look nice to impress others, or over-complicated to use.

It can be hand-written, or on a computer spreadsheet — it makes no difference to its effectiveness.

57. Get A System

It is important to ensure you allocate time to tasks and actions that are *important*, before they become *urgent*. If these tasks are not scheduled into an action plan and time set-aside for their completion, then it is unlikely that your goal stands much chance of being achieved. If you have defined some actions as being neither urgent nor important, you should seriously consider if they need doing at all.

"The key is not to prioritise what's on your schedule, but to schedule your priorities."
Stephen R. Covey

You might not be able to control your daily workload or schedule, but you can plan your priorities each day. A prioritised daily task list is more effective than a *to do list*, although it is still not sufficient to enable you to achieve larger Go MAD goals. Often uncompleted actions from one day get carried forward to the next, or the list becomes one of prioritised urgent actions. Somehow, you need a way of ensuring that time gets spent on the important, but non-urgent actions.

Prioritise the actions from your list that you have defined as important. Start with those that are important and urgent, and sort them into an order of priority. Notice the critical path i.e. actions that have to happen in a specific order to allow other actions to happen. Now allocate time in your diary or planner to start or complete these important actions. If at this point you don't have a diary or planner, I suggest you get one. The only way to ensure that important tasks are included in daily task lists is to plan them in before the day starts.

"It is useless to desire more time, if you are already wasting what little you have."
James Allen

Using a planning system should help you, as it has me, to increase your efficiency by at least 10%. This will give you six minutes each hour, or an extra 60 minutes every ten hours, to Go MAD. One hour each day is the equivalent of 5 weeks over the course of a year. Remember: this is not time saved; it is time that can be spent on whatever you choose to Go MAD about.

58. Clear Out The Clutter

If you are to reallocate some of your time to doing things that are important in moving you towards your worthwhile goal, you will need to stop doing some of the things that you currently spend your time on. The easiest place to start is with the non-important things that clutter your life.

TIME TO WRITE

On the next page, identify things that currently occupy your time and are less important than pursuing your worthwhile goal.

Non-important things that I currently spend my valuable time on:

-
-
-
-
-
-
-

-
-
-
-
-
-
-

Are you in a comfortable rut with any of these things?

Is the comfortable rut stronger than your reason why?

What actions would you have to take to stop doing some of these non-important things, and Go MAD instead?

Which of these actions are you prepared to take?

59. Notice The Time Stealers

Several years ago, my credit cards, driving licence and £80 cash were stolen from my wallet, in a hotel where I was staying. The circumstances were outside of my control; it was a *given*, and hence all I could do was react calmly in response to the situation. It was an inconvenience, but I could get new cards and apply for another licence.

This inconvenience took approximately five hours in total, including phone calls, letters and making a police statement. This time had been lost from my schedule. The stolen items would eventually be replaced; the stolen time will never be replaced.

"Does thou love life? Then do not squander time,
for that is the stuff life is made of."
Benjamin Franklin

Whilst I was aware that my time was being stolen, it was very much a given; urgent tasks had to be completed. Often this is not the case, and valuable time is stolen by other people without you noticing. Start to question the importance of interruptions that demand your urgent time and attention.

TIME TO THINK

Who do you allow to steal your time?

For what purpose do they steal it?

Does this conflict with your core values?

60. Learn From The Past; Apply To The Future

The following two activities are to help you gain additional insight about the actions that will be critical in ensuring you Go MAD They both involve using your imagination.

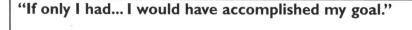

TIME TO THINK

Remind yourself of the timescale of your goal. Now imagine that you have travelled forward in time and reached that specific date by which you aimed to achieve your goal. However, the goal has not been achieved by this time. To help your imagination you might want to close your eyes and notice what you see; what you can hear, and what you feel are the reasons for not achieving the goal. Now complete the following sentence:

> **"If only I had... I would have accomplished my goal."**

Return to the present and consider your answers. What did you realise? Revisit your action plan and amend as appropriate to ensure any necessary actions are included.

TIME TO THINK AGAIN

Using the same goal and timescale, imagine reaching the specific date again, but this time imagine achieving your goal. Use your imagination to discover the reason for your success. What can you see, hear and feel that provide clues?

I achieved my goal because...

-

-

-

-

-

Take note of any further actions you need to include in your plan.

61. Understand That The Plan Will Change

Imagine a ship that sets sail on an important journey. It has a specific destination to reach by a certain date and a detailed plan of how to get there. As it travels towards its distant journey's end, the captain steers the ship continually making adjustments to keep it on course. It gains speed in good wind conditions and slows down in rough seas. The captain regularly checks the position of the vessel, refers to the navigation charts, consults with others, and notes progress in the ship's logbook.

Have a firm goal and a flexible plan.

Plan, but don't over plan. You will need to make adjustments to take advantage of opportunities that emerge, or to overcome temporary setbacks. Remember the plan is not the goal.

Give yourself a deadline to stop planning and to start taking action. As you involve others (principle five) the plan will change, so plan to review your plan at regular intervals.

TIME TO REFLECT

Having reached the end of this section, consider the following questions:

What has prevented me in the past from effectively planning my priorities?

How much time will I set aside for future possibility thinking?

What are the elements and the format of my action plan?

What method will I use to ensure I action my priorities?

What are the most important actions I need to plan time for?

How can I make better use of my time to Go MAD?

What have I learned about Go MAD Principle Three?

What are the implications?

What do I want to do differently?

Principle Four

HAVE SELF-BELIEF

THAT YOU

CAN AND WILL

GO MAD

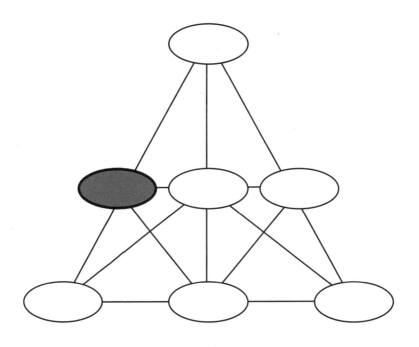

"I know this now. Every man gives his life for what he believes. Every woman gives her life for what she believes. Sometimes people believe in little or nothing, yet give their lives to that little or nothing. One life is all we have and we live it as we believe in living it. And then it is gone. But to sacrifice what you are and live without belief, that's more terrible than dying."
Joan of Arc

62. Answer Two Questions

TIME TO THINK

Your answers to the following questions will reveal much about your current level of self-belief.

> **What do you believe is the realistic probability of your defined goal being achieved within the set timescale?**
>
> **To what extent do you see yourself as having the necessary ability and confidence to succeed?**

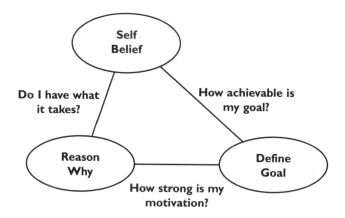

The "internal triangle" of the Go MAD® Framework

"Your future will be a reflection of the components of your current thinking – the questions you ask yourself, the statements you make inside your head, the memories you recall and the future you imagine. The thoughts that dominate your mind will either help or hinder your progress. You choose."
Andy Gilbert

Self-belief is important in making a difference; it generates energy and helps you to build on your strong reason why, to maintain momentum. It is also essential when involving others (principle 5); if you don't believe in yourself or grow your goal, how can you expect others to? When you believe in your ability to Go MAD, your mind uses its creative powers and becomes solution focused.

"You are not what you think you are.
But what you think - YOU ARE!"
Dr. Norman Vincent Peale

---

63. Strengthen Your Belief In Your Ability To Achieve

It's all in the mind – in fact, it's mainly about what you think and say to yourself. Hence, the following sections are all aimed at helping you to understand ways of controlling your mind for the benefit of yourself. Some of the ideas and methods build upon the earlier part of this book, where I described the importance of your subconscious mind and using imagination. You might find it useful to refer back to this, in sections 37-42.

Remember that your subconscious mind records all the information you receive and think about, even as you read this book. Repetition of positive messages to yourself is a fundamental way of increasing your self-belief. So, as you continue to read about how to make a difference, keep reminding yourself, "*I can make a difference; I will make a difference; I am already making a difference; I make a difference.*"

"Whether you believe you can or you can't,
you are right."
Henry Ford

You have the ability to leave a lasting impression in your own mind. Make it a positive one; an enabling self-belief.

64. Invest In Your Greatest Asset

Have you seen the film "Pretty Woman"? Richard Gere plays the part of a businessman who hires a prostitute, played by Julia Roberts, as his escort to impress business clients. At one point, he tells her what a great person she is. She replies, "The bad stuff is easier to believe," after commenting, "If people put you down enough, you start to believe it."

To what extent do you believe in yourself? If you see yourself as a successful person with the ability and confidence to succeed: you will succeed. This mental picture you have of yourself is sometimes referred to as your *self-image*. Your self-image influences everything you do. When your self-image is in line with your goal; your goal is more likely to be achieved.

People tend not to believe what they see.
Instead, they see what they believe.

The opinion you have of yourself creates your self-image. It is formed by what you say to yourself and whether or not you accept what others say about you. This opinion, plus your abilities, will cause you to feel either confident or insecure.

65. Be Your Own Best Friend

Many people have a poor self-image and opinion of themselves. Very often, this is continually reinforced by the internal repetitious messages they give themselves:

"I'm no good at..."
"I'm hopeless at..."
"I can't do..."
"I'm awful at..."
"I'm clumsy; stupid; thick, etc."
"I'm useless at..."

"I'll never do it."

Imagine your best friend spoke to you out loud in the same way as you speak to yourself, would he, or she, be saying:

"You're great at..."	or	"You're no good at…"
"You're fantastic at…"		"You're hopeless at…"
"You're so talented at..."		"You'll never do it..."
"You're confident at…"		"You're clumsy, stupid, thick, etc."

You probably wouldn't want to associate with someone who continually gave you such hindering messages. Your best friend would soon become your ex-friend. However, you might not realise the potential damage that hindering *self-talk* can cause. You have the opportunity to become your own best friend by programming your mind with helpful messages. The subconscious mind accepts and believes exactly what passes through the conscious mind.

TIME TO REFLECT

Up until now, have you been your own best friend, or your own worst enemy? What messages have you been giving yourself? Are they helpful or hindering?

Hindering messages (to be replaced)	Helpful messages (to be continued)
-	-
-	-
-	-

66. Learn To Like Yourself Even More

Start by appreciating what you like about yourself. What are your good points; your personal qualities and attributes that will enable you to Go MAD?

TIME TO WRITE

Write a list.

I am...	I like my...
I am...	I like my...
I am...	I like my...
I am...	I like my...

67. Sell Yourself To Yourself

If you had to design an advert for yourself that described your skills, abilities, talents and achievements, what would it say?

TIME TO REFLECT

Notice your internal self-talk relating to the previous sentence. What are you telling yourself about yourself? How helpful is it? What are the implications?

**"Your self-talk affects your beliefs,
your beliefs affect your capability,
your capability affects your actions,
your actions affect your results."
Andy Gilbert**

Whatever your reaction to this exercise, be very aware that your subconscious mind is recording it. If you choose to take time and design an advert for yourself, here are a few tips:

- Develop an initial list of your skills, abilities, talents and achievements.
- Select several that you want to describe in more detail.
- Blow your own trumpet, and make them sound great.
- Have fun, and lavish praise upon yourself in your description.
- Read the advert to yourself – not to other people!

TIME TO WRITE

An advert for myself:

68. Reinforce The Beliefs You Desire

The subconscious mind cannot distinguish between real and imagined events, or truth and untruth; that is the job of the conscious mind. The subconscious mind just accepts the messages it receives. Therefore, it is possible to trick your subconscious into recording information, deliberately passed by your conscious mind, which is untrue. This can be really helpful if you want to develop a belief that you do not have.

You can achieve more than you currently believe.

When I decided to make a difference about my health and fitness, I obviously applied Go MAD to help me think about my reason why, my defined goals, possibilities and my plan of priorities (principles one to three). When I examined my self-belief, I realised I needed to do two things. Firstly, I needed to break my end goal down into small sub-goals that I believed were achievable. Secondly, I needed to change an existing belief that was hindering my ability to succeed.

The belief I had was that I enjoyed eating big portions of food. Ironically, I had not developed this belief through a love of food. Instead, I had allowed it to develop in my subconscious mind through my sense of humour. Let me explain. As I regularly work away from home, running development programmes, I often eat in restaurants. At mealtimes, I am invariably with a group of people and as the menu is discussed, someone usually asks, "What are you having to eat?" to which my standard reply was, "Big portions!" Over the years, I had said this phrase so many times that it had become a belief: a belief that had become a reality. It needed to be changed if I was to make a difference.

**"When the will and imagination are in conflict,
it is always the imagination that wins."
Emile Coué**

I started to reprogramme my mind with two new self-belief statements that I considered more helpful and in line with achieving my goal:

"I enjoy eating healthy food."
"I am getting slimmer and slimmer every day."

It is important to note that at the time I did not believe either of these statements to be true. However, I understood how the subconscious mind would help me and that repetition was the key. I deliberately used both statements as often as I could to start with. I said them to myself as self-talk whenever I thought about food and also said them out loud.

"Our aspirations are our possibilities."
Robert Browning

When working in the office, I would decline any sweets or biscuits on offer and enjoy saying my statements out loud. Kathryn, Ian and the rest of the team even started to say, "It's no use offering Andy a sweet because he only enjoys eating healthy food." This was great news, as now the message was being reinforced in my own mind by the comments of others!

After approximately three weeks, I noticed that I was consciously saying these statements less often. However, now I actually believed them. By this time, I must have said each statement at least 100 times; I was enjoying eating healthy food, and I was getting slimmer. I now had the self-belief that would enable me to achieve my end goal.

69. Writing Helpful Self-Talk Statements

You cannot short-circuit your self-belief when seeking to Go MAD. In other words, you cannot programme your subconscious mind with goals if your conscious mind does not believe they are possible to achieve. Any thoughts or feelings of self-doubt will, of course, also be recognised and recorded by the subconscious mind.

The following tips will help you to use self-talk statements effectively:

- Phrase your statement in the present tense as if it is already happening, e.g. "I am..." or, "I enjoy..."

- Put emotion into your statement e.g. "I feel *great* exercising twice weekly."

- Start with easy statements to get used to using them.

- Write your statements on small cards and use them as a reminder.

- Review them in the morning, throughout the day and at night.

- Remember that self-talk statements are not always true when you start using them. The mind only has to believe that they can become true.

- Replace them with new ones, once they have served their purpose.

TIME TO WRITE

Practise writing a few helpful self-talk statements by completing the following sentences.

> **I am...**
>
> **I enjoy...**
>
> **Everyday I...**
>
> **I feel great...**

If you use carefully worded self-talk statements for 21-30 days, and review them three times daily, you will notice the difference.

70. Reap What You Sow

Your mind is like a fertile patch of earth where you can choose what to plant. Sow helpful thoughts and reap good results; sow hindering thoughts and reap poor results. You can choose what thoughts you sow. You can also choose what you read; what you watch on television, and what music you listen to.

"You don't achieve happiness by focusing on things that make you unhappy."
Andy Gilbert

The power of how easily the subconscious mind stores information and influences your behaviour can be illustrated very simply. Have you ever found yourself humming, singing or whistling a tune without consciously realising? Incredibly, you know the words and the melody although you have not consciously learnt them. All this information has been stored through repetitive programming that you have not been aware of! "I can't get this tune out of my head," or "I've got this song on my brain" are very true statements.

"Don't listen to what they say. Go see."
Chinese proverb

What is it that makes you believe that one brand or product is better than the next? Advertisers understand the power of repetition on the subconscious mind. Wouldn't it be great, if the stuff you couldn't get out of your head, was helpful thoughts you had deliberately planted; thoughts which had now blossomed into enabling beliefs. Feed your mind with belief and help it to grow.

71. Create Your Own Reality

The Russian Olympian weightlifter Vasily Alexeev, had lifted 499 pounds, but could not break a weight-lifting record of 500 pounds.

He had made many unsuccessful attempts. Eventually his trainer put 501.5 pounds on the bar but made it look like 499 pounds. He lifted it easily; the limit he had set himself existed only in his mind. Other weightlifters went on to break his record, because they now believed it possible to lift 500 pounds.

Beliefs are not facts.

Our research provided many day-to-day examples of how people who made a difference, created their own reality. Many commented about overcoming a lack of self-belief by "telling myself I could do it." Others commented that they had initially created "barriers in my own mind," before realising their limiting beliefs.

**Beliefs are your current reality and
not necessarily your future.**

Albert Einstein   -   didn't speak until age 4.
                 -   couldn't read until age 7.
                 -   was described by one teacher as "mentally slow, unsociable, and adrift forever in his foolish dreams."
                 -   was expelled from a college and refused admission to another.

Colonel Sanders -   worked for 40 years as a railroad labourer.
                 -   visited nearly 500 restaurants in an attempt to sell his Kentucky Fried Chicken recipe, and was aged 65 when he succeeded.

TIME TO THINK

Ask yourself:

> **Is my current thinking helpful or hindering?**
>
> **Which of the four thinking components (self-talk statements, questions I ask myself, recalled memories or imagined future) is hindering?**
>
> **If I was to choose to change that hindering component of my thinking to something more helpful, what could that possibly be?**

72. Recognise The Possible Source Of Your Hindering Beliefs

Beliefs that either help or hinder your ability to Go MAD, have been developed during the course of your life. Comments made by parents, guardians, schoolteachers, peers, work colleagues and managers might all have made a deep impact on your subconscious mind.

I have known many people who can recall their parents consistently calling them, "stupid," or "clumsy," and have grown up believing it to be true. I also hear adults repeatedly programming their children's minds with negative criticism that will eventually turn into a hindering self-belief. The majority of children never develop the conscious ability to filter out or disregard these comments and hence these can become hindering self-beliefs.

"You are never too old; never too young to make a difference. Age is not a barrier unless you allow it to be."
Andy Gilbert

If you have identified any hindering beliefs about your ability to pursue, and achieve, the difference you desire, then take heart: beliefs can change. You can change them – if you have a strong enough reason why.

Change your beliefs and you change your reality.

Limiting beliefs have existed throughout history:

"The world is flat" – but Christopher Columbus made a difference.

"Germs and bacteria don't exist" – until Louis Pasteur proved they did.

"Men can't fly" – but the Wright Brothers maintained their self-belief.

In 1927, Harry Warner of Warner Bros. Pictures commented, "Who the hell wants to hear actors talk?"

In the 1960s who believed that personal computers would exist?

In the 1970s who believed the internet was possible?

In the 1980s who believed that footballers could earn over £80,000 per week?

As a child did you believe in Father Christmas or the Tooth Fairy?

TIME TO REFLECT

What hindering beliefs have I already changed?

What do I now believe is possible for me to achieve?

73. Keep Your Dreams Alive

Recognise the *dream stealers*. These people tell you that you will not achieve your goals. Recognise that they are sharing their hindering beliefs. Filter them out of your mind by consciously deciding not to accept their comments as reality. It often helps to consider what, if anything, that person has achieved or accomplished in their life that qualifies them to attempt to set limitations for you. People who say it can't be done are usually unsuccessful in setting or achieving worthwhile goals for themselves.

"Imagination is more important than knowledge."
Albert Einstein

Every difference ever made, first started in someone's imagination. Increase your self-belief by imagining in detail the difference you desire. Dreams need to be built, then built upon again and allowed to grow. Visions and aspirations need to be underpinned with tangible goals.

TIME TO REFLECT

Has the difference I want to make ever been achieved by someone else?

Who would I consider to be a good role model?

Has anyone else with less ability than me ever succeeded in making a difference?

Could this difference be achieved by anyone else?

If they can, so can you.

74. Choose Your Thoughts

Imagine your mind is a television with only two channels; channel helpful and channel hindering. Which channel do you tune into the most? Many people have programmed their mind to tune in automatically to channel hindering without realising. Have you ever got up in the morning, looked outside at the weather and made a comment like, "What a terrible day, I might as well go back to bed"? Have you ever met someone who has said, "I knew when I got up this morning, that it would be a bad day"?

Your thoughts can create a self-fulfilling prophecy that you might be unaware of. The circumstances might be a *given* – like the weather being outside your control – but how you choose to react to the circumstances is for you to decide.

Every coin has two sides. Develop the habit of looking at the flipside. Your conscious mind can only hold one thought at a time; helpful or hindering. It's your choice; which will it be? If your goal is worthwhile, it makes sense to choose helpful thoughts to support your progress towards achieving it.

**"It's not the cards you are dealt,
but how you play your hand."
Winifred Gilbert**

My Grandmother taught me to play cards when I was a young boy. I sometimes used to comment, "It's not fair! You've got all the good cards." She always reminded me that, "A good card-player never blames the cards. He always makes the most of his hand." We then used to practise playing the same game, again and again. Not surprisingly, I have developed a high self-belief about my card playing ability!

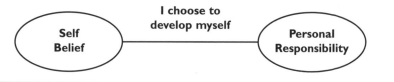

**"Feeling sorry for yourself and your present condition
is not only a waste of energy,
but the worst habit you could possibly have."
Dale Carnegie**

You can choose to develop your confidence and your abilities. Go MAD principle six focuses on taking personal responsibility for your own development.

TIME TO THINK

What are the circumstances that, in the past, I have allowed to negatively influence my thinking about the differences that I want to make?

75. Release Unnecessary Fears

It has been estimated that up to 96% of your worries and fears are unnecessary.

40% of worries never happen,
30% of worries are from the past,
12% of worries are groundless health concerns,
10% of worries are relatively petty,
8% of worries are real, but half of these (4% of the total) are out of your control.

"We have nothing to fear, except fear itself."
Franklin Roosevelt

I don't know if these figures are true or not, but they might make you think about how much time you spend worrying unnecessarily. Worries attract more worries, as your mind attracts what it thinks about. Choose not to spend time on them – Go MAD instead! People who make a difference have just as many real worries, but they certainly have fewer imaginary ones!

**"Do the thing you fear to do
and you will find the power to do it."**
Earl Nightingale

Babies are born with only two fears; loud noises and falling – all other fears are learned. Fear of failure is therefore a learned response and can be overcome. However, many people, imagine their fears happening in vivid detail. Remember that the subconscious mind cannot tell the difference between real and imagined events.

F.E.A.R. is False Expectations Appearing Real

There are many good books, audio CD's and development

programmes that provide more detailed information and guidance about overcoming fear and developing confidence. Visit a good quality bookstore and have a browse through the personal development section – but only if you have a strong enough reason why.

An activity, I often use with people who appear to be unnecessarily worrying is to ask them to define their worry or fear in writing. If you have identified any such issue, which might affect your ability to Go MAD, you might want to consider the following exercise.

TIME TO WRITE

Use a separate sheet of paper and write down your problem in specific detail.

Break it down into identifiable chunks.

List possible options and ways forward (set yourself a target of at least 10-20 options).

Leave the list for a couple of days.

Relax and allow your subconscious mind to suggest solutions.

76. Eliminate Failure

Failure is only an option if you let it be. Every action produces a result, although it might not be the desired result. You choose your response to this result. Using the word *failure* is not helpful. Nobody likes to be called a failure by others, so why describe yourself that way? The reason why so many people believe they are failures is because that message has been repeatedly imprinted on their minds.

"No one can keep you down, except yourself."
Andy Gilbert

Choose to eliminate this word from your mind by replacing it with a word or phrase that is more helpful; e.g. result; feedback; learning experience; temporary setback, or discovery. Thomas Edison reportedly made approximately 10,000 attempts before successfully inventing electric light. He was asked what it was like to fail so many times, and replied, "I did not fail, I simply discovered thousands of ways that wouldn't produce light."

77. Become Solution Focused

If you look for problems, you will find problems; if you look for solutions, you will find solutions. You get what you focus on.

I have a massive library of books and development materials that I often lend to friends and clients. I am always amused when people focus on what they didn't like about a book or an audio CD, "It's too American," or, "I didn't like the sound of his voice."

"Don't let what you don't like,
get in the way of what you might discover."
Andy Gilbert

Remember the *supermarket shopping trolley approach:* gather what you want and leave behind what you don't.

78. Increase Your Options

If you want more choice, then consider more options.

TIME TO THINK

Outlined on the next page are ways to maintain or develop your self-belief to a level that will enable you to Go MAD. Decide which combination of these will help you the most.

- Regularly celebrate small successes and the achievement of sub-goals.
- Associate more with people who are positive; mix less with those who are negative.
- Identify and meet role models who have achieved what you want to achieve.
- Visualise your goals being successfully achieved – by you.
- Persist in pursuing your goal.

It's not the method, it's the mindset.

- Develop and use positive self-talk statements.
- Avoid unhealthy comparisons. It's what *you* do that's important.
- Read positive, developmental books.
- Be decisive (indecision leads to doubt, which leads to fear).
- Reduce and eliminate worries by defining them, and generating solutions.
- Recreate in your mind past experiences of success.
- Dress for success - look good and feel good.

"I will act as if what I do makes a difference."
William James

- Change any negative images in your mind.
- Learn to like yourself even more.
- Identify hindering thoughts and work towards replacing them with helpful thoughts.
- Be aware of your self-talk and the messages you give yourself.
- Recognise your strengths, abilities and personal qualities.
- Focus on what you want and regularly review your goals.
- Identify sources of positive energy.
- Remind yourself of past achievements.

"Happiness doesn't depend on what we have,
but it does depend on how we feel
towards what we have.
We can be happy with little
and miserable with much."
W. D. Hoard

TIME TO REFLECT

Having reached the end of this section, consider the two
questions that you were asked at the start:

**What do I believe is the realistic probability of my
defined goal being achieved within the set timescale?**

**To what extent do I see myself as having the necessary
ability and confidence to succeed?**

Now consider:

**What realisations have I had about Go MAD Principle
Four?**

What are the implications?

What do I want to consider doing differently?

What do I want to continue doing successfully?

"**Anyone who stops learning is old,
whether twenty or eighty.
Anyone who keeps learning is young.
The greatest thing in life
is to keep your mind young.**"
Henry Ford

Principle Five

INVOLVE OTHERS

TO HELP YOU

GO MAD

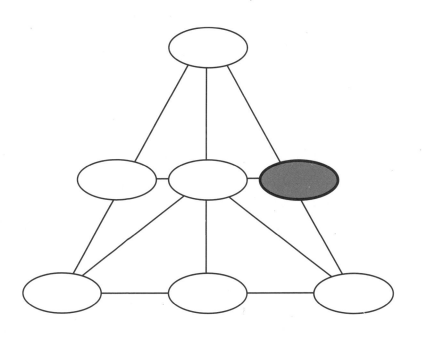

**If you want to know
the way up the mountain,
ask someone
who has travelled the road.**

79. Plan Before Involving Others

The greater the difference you want to make, the greater the potential for involving others. Your success will depend upon how effectively you gain the involvement of others to agree, implement, accept or take numerous other actions.

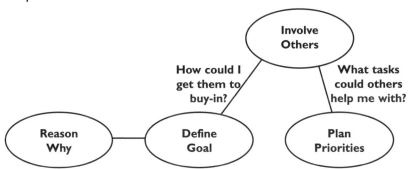

Your defined goal is linked to *your* reason why. Notice in the above diagram that *your* reason why (principle one), is not directly linked to principle five. The goal acts as a vehicle to satisfy *your* reason for wanting to Go MAD. In order to involve others, you need to gain their commitment. The link in the Go MAD Framework between the defined goal and involving others is referred to as the 'buy-in' line. It includes everything to do with communicating your goal to others and influencing them to take action to help you.

This means you need to consider the needs of others you seek to involve. What are *their* motives for action; *their* similar or conflicting goals; *their* current priorities; *their* likely levels of belief in your goal; *their* self-belief in their own ability, and *their* perceptions of you? These are questions you need to consider when planning who to involve and how to involve them.

Other people will not Go MAD about achieving a goal given to them by someone else, unless they have a strong enough reason why and believe it is achievable. Your role is to ensure they do – by involving them.

80. Have A Reason For Their Involvement

Think about the many possible reasons for involving others and how they could help you. Then think about who you could possibly involve. These are two of the ten possibility thinking areas mentioned earlier in section 54.

TIME TO THINK

Focus on the difference you want to make and use the following list to stimulate your thinking about possible reasons for involving others. Add any further reasons you have identified.

- They have useful knowledge, or access to it.
- They have specialist skills.
- They have done it before.
- They can influence other key people.
- They can help you to gain access to other key people.
- They are key decision-makers.
- They can involve other people.
- They have an interest in the outcome.
- To save time.
- To generate ideas.
- To have fun.
- To gain credibility.
- To maintain organisational politics.
- To complete tasks.
- To help organise.
- For support - emotional; financial; resources; etc.
- As a sounding board to bounce ideas off.
- To develop their skills, knowledge, behaviour, self-belief.
- To gain alternative viewpoints.
- To learn from their experience.
- To keep the dream alive.
- To maintain momentum.
- To reduce their resistance to change.

- To improve your action planning.
- To give you feedback about progress.
- To steer you back on course.
- Other reasons...

81. Decide Who To Involve

There are so many people who could potentially help if you approach them in the right way: friends, teachers, colleagues, customers, family, social acquaintances, business contacts, experts and many others. Consider involving:

- Your partner
- People with a similar goal
- People with shared core values
- People inside and outside your peer group
- People of higher and lower status or authority
- People you admire

It is also possible to involve others without ever meeting or knowing them. The knowledge and experience of others can be gained from books and a wide range of audio/visual material. This is an easy way of getting access to new information that will help you to Go MAD.

**"Intelligence is not the ability to store information,
but to know where to find it."
Albert Einstein**

Internet access to the World Wide Web opens up a variety of options for involving others: access and download information from websites; subscribe to specialist forums; ask for help on bulletin boards, and send information via e-mail.

82. Think Carefully Before Sharing Your Goal

Of the people you are considering involving, assess who is likely to be the most supportive. If you are looking to involve a large number of people, think about the order in which you will approach them.

Recognise that whilst your goal should be clearly understandable to others, your reason why might not be. You need to consider how you can most effectively explain and help others understand the importance of the goal to you. Remember, also, that to be effective in involving others, you should go way beyond just stating the facts. A variety of research has shown that you can influence people easier by explaining the reason why at the same time as sharing the defined goal. The following six sections explain this further.

83. Walk In The Shoes Of Others

Everyone is different, with different needs and motivations. You need to be able to look at the differences from their point of view, to discover their possible reasons for becoming involved. By considering how they are likely to feel and react to you, your goal and the difference you intend to make, you will gain valuable insight into *how* to gain their involvement.

There is an old North American Indian piece of wisdom that advises: "In order to fully understand another person you need to walk in their moccasins."

TIME TO THINK

Focus on someone who you want to involve in helping you to Go MAD.

1. Imagine stepping out of your shoes and into theirs for a while. Imagine being in their position and doing the things that they do in their environment. What do you see? What do you hear? How does it feel?

2. See things as if looking through their eyes. What do you notice about how they view you? What do you look like? What do they focus on?

3. How do they feel about you; about your ideas and suggestions; about your requests for assistance, and about the way you help them?

4. Listen through their ears. What do you notice about the way you speak; your tone of voice and the words you use when seeking to involve them?

This exercise takes a bit of practice, in order to really be able to walk for a while in the shoes of someone else. You might find it easier to do with your eyes closed.

Make a note below of any insights that will help you in the future.

84. Recognise Their Reason Why

TIME TO THINK

What is in it for them?

Why should they be bothered?

What are their core values?

What are they passionate about?

85. Understand Their Goals And Dreams

Others are not likely to have their goals as well defined as you – if they have any goals at all. Instead, they might have some aims, aspirations or hopes – or not. Seek to understand what is important to them, before explaining what is important to you. Discover clues that you can refer back to when involving them. Listening builds trust and trust builds relationships.

Build bridges, not barriers.

Experienced anglers are skilled in identifying, and baiting their hooks with, what the fish prefer. Different fish, in different rivers, at different times, want different food. To hook the imagination and capture the involvement of others, spend time assessing what they want.

86. Give More To Receive More

Others are more likely to help you achieve your goals if you have already given help to them. The best way to get co-operation is to give co-operation. Help others to be successful in achieving their goals and you will receive the support you require. Keep in touch on an ongoing basis with those you might want to involve, not just when you want their help.

**"Those who give little, receive little;
those who give more, receive more."
Andy Gilbert**

By doing this you will also discover more about how the Go MAD key principles are applied by others. This will enable you to build genuine win-win relationships – where both you and others benefit – that work towards achieving mutually satisfying goals.

87. Develop Likeable Qualities

You are a sales person. I realise that this is a term you might not relate to – notice your internal self-talk that is already programming your subconscious mind – but it's true. You sell yourself daily to others. They may not pay you with money, but they do give their valuable time. When seeking to involve others in your goal you are competing with many other things to attract their time and attention.

I read some research that mentioned over 80% of sales are based upon the customer liking the salesperson. So how likeable are you? How attractive are your qualities to other people? Whilst different people like different qualities, most people like others who are honest, friendly, helpful, trustworthy, supportive, hard working, appreciative, and positive. You can probably identify other qualities of people you like to be involved with.

> **TIME TO WRITE**

On the next page, identify likeable qualities of people who you enjoy helping and being involved with.

Likeable qualities of others
-         -
-         -
-         -
-         -
-         -

Now consider the viewpoint of other people, and identify how they perceive your qualities – likeable and unlikeable! It might help to re-read section 83 and walk in the shoes of others for a while.

My likeable qualities	My not so likeable qualities
-	-
-	-
-	-
-	-
-	-

Remind yourself of the three different types of goal from section 32. In order to have, or to be able to do, something, you might first need to become more effective. The skill of involving others and the development of likeable qualities might become areas to Go MAD about – if you have a strong enough reason why, of course!

> ## "He who can copy, can do."
> ## Leonardo De Vinci

88. Work To Gain Support

You now need to consider how to involve others and gain their support. In doing this, be aware of the impact of your influencing skills:

- Express your desire and reason why in the way you speak. Let your enthusiasm inspire others. Show how important your goal is.
- Make others feel important and explain why you would like them involved.
- Ensure you communicate how others will benefit from making a difference. Show how important your goal is.
- Ask directly for their involvement, rather than telling or assuming their support.
- Demonstrate your likeable qualities.
- Encourage others to ask questions and comment.
- Value people's time and thank them for their involvement as progress is made – not just when the goal is achieved.
- Ask for opinions, ideas and suggestions.
- Be prepared to redefine your goal, re-prioritise and re-plan your priorities, if appropriate.
- Treat others, as you know they would like to be treated (having walked in their shoes).
- Share the credit for your success with those who have been involved.

> ## "A wise man creates more opportunities than he finds."
> ## Francis Bacon

TIME TO REFLECT

Having reached the end of this section, consider the following questions:

How could others possibly help me?

Who do I want to involve?

How do I want to involve them?

What is the reason why they would want to be involved?

How could I possibly gain their buy-in?

What could I possibly do to help them?

How do others perceive me?

What interpersonal skills or personal qualities do I need to further develop?

What was the most important aspect of Go MAD Principle Five that I realised?

Principle Six

TAKE

PERSONAL

RESPONSIBILITY

FOR YOUR ACTIONS

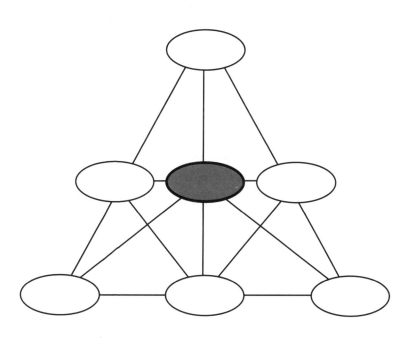

"**People are always blaming circumstances
for what they are.
I don't believe in circumstances.
The people who get on in this world
are the people who get up and
look for the circumstances they want,
and if they can't find them,
they make them.**"
George Bernard Shaw

89. Use The World's Greatest Expert

You are the world's greatest expert about *you* making a difference.

You have incredible insider knowledge about your motivation, your capabilities, your dreams, and your ambitions. No one else knows as much about you, as you do. No one else has as great a stake in your future as you do.

**If you want to make a difference,
YOU have got to make the difference.**

It's not what you know that's important; it's what you do with it, that matters. Taking responsibility for your actions and the choices you have made in the past, is the first step. The second step, is to take responsibility for your current situation and your future. Choosing to apply the Go MAD key principles is a decision *you* have to make.

**"I am free to be what I want to be and
to do what I want to do."
Richard Bach**

The only person who can determine your success is you. Decide to use your incredible potential to Go MAD about whatever is important enough for *you*.

90. Refuse To Blame Others Or Make Excuses

I have worked with over 100 organisations during the past ten years. In many there is a high level of blame; with people at one level, blaming people at another; people in one team, blaming people in other teams; people blaming each other; people blaming the weather, the heavy traffic – the examples are endless. What positive use does it serve in making a difference? None at all – a classic case of whining dog syndrome – just letting everyone else know about an uncomfortable situation without doing anything productive about it.

"Don't curse the darkness – light a candle."
Chinese Proverb

What's more, many managers I meet proudly claim that, "We don't have a blame culture here." Notice how the word *blame* gets programmed into the mind once more. What would be more helpful is to focus on what they want, which is the opposite i.e. a *responsibility* culture. However, many people seem to prefer blaming rather than taking responsibility. Go MAD about this!

It is liberating to say, "I take responsibility for… (your actions)," either out loud or to yourself, as a positive affirmation. Even when admitting mistakes and taking responsibility, still speak positively and question yourself, "What could I have done more effectively, or differently?"

Remember that your subconscious mind accepts the messages it receives, as true. When blaming others, your subconscious mind acts on this belief to prove that it is the fault of someone else. Hence, nothing happens to change the pattern of your behaviour. Whereas, taking responsibility and seeking to learn as a result of your actions, causes your mind to start automatically adjusting your behaviour to become more responsible.

"Our greatest glory is not in never falling,
but in rising every time we fall."
Confucius

---

91. Don't Use Estate Agents

At least if you do use them, don't blame or use them as an excuse for your house not being sold. Now, before you get the wrong idea, I believe that estate agents provide a valuable service – if *you* don't want to take responsibility for selling your house.

If you want to Go MAD about selling your house, you need to recognise that involving estate agents (principle five) is just one possibility. I have helped several friends to sell their houses in the past couple of years, by enabling them to take responsibility for their actions.

Earlier this year someone commented to me, "I've tried everything to sell my house," and he then went on to blame various factors and people.

Noticing immediately that he had only been *trying*. I decided to challenge the *everything* and have some fun. I asked him, "You've tried everything? What were the last 40 things you *tried?*"

"I haven't tried 40 things."

"OK what about the 30 ways you've tried?"
"What do you mean 30 ways?"

"20 ways? 10 ways? 5 ways? What things have you tried?" I eventually asked.

"Well it's been on with the estate agents for the last 12 months!"

> **"Be absolutely clear about what you want,**
> **why you want it, when you want it**
> **and what you are willing to do to get it."**
> **Brian Tracy**

A few years ago, I found my dream house. Seven people viewed the property the same day, and I knew I had to act quickly. The challenge was that I had not sold my own house – in fact, it was not even up for sale! I needed to move fast and take personal responsibility for my actions: the goal was to find a buyer in the next five days. I involved family and friends to brainstorm over 40 ideas, and we planned priorities. I had total self-belief that my goal was possible to achieve; it was down to me, and I took action. Within 36 hours, I had a cash-buyer for my house; within 48 hours my offer was accepted, and two months later we moved into our dream house.

"If you dream it, you can do it."
Walt Disney

---

92. Lead By Example

Your words and actions influence the behaviour and attitudes of others. Talking about making a difference and actually doing it are two separate things. Many of the people we interviewed specifically commented on the importance of being a role model for others and leading by example. *Personal leadership* is a term that aptly describes your role in using Go MAD to achieve results. When you become the leader, you must accept responsibility for the outcome of your actions.

"Be willing to do what others are not.
There are no traffic jams on that extra mile!"
Andy Gilbert

TIME TO THINK

In three, five or ten years time, today's future will arrive. Will you have taken responsibility to be where you want to be? What will you say to yourself when the time arrives?

Are you a role model to others around you?

Could you be the inspiration to help others Go MAD?

93. Exercise Your Power To Choose

I hope, by now, you have realised that you can learn to take greater control of your mind. Your mind is like a magnet; more powerful than any other magnet. You *choose* what to attract and how to react to the givens. The decisions are yours and yours alone. You can choose to take responsibility and consciously apply the key principles, or you can choose not to. Exercising your power to choose is at the core of key principle six and provides the links with each of the first five Go MAD key principles.

- Reason why – choosing if you can be bothered or not.
- Define goal – choosing what success means for you and by what date.
- Plan priorities – choosing how much time to spend on what activities.
- Self-belief – choosing to develop yourself.
- Involving others – choosing who to involve and how to involve them.

"To Go MAD or not to Go MAD
that is the question.
Whether 'tis nobler in the mind to suffer
the slings and arrows of outrageous fortune,
or to Go MAD about a sea of troubles,
and by taking responsibility, end them?"
Adapted from William Shakespeare

The following seven sections refer back to the first five key principles and examine the choices you face in deciding whether, or not, to Go MAD. Further guidance is also given in developing your ability to do so.

94. Choose To Move On

You decide how to travel through life. You choose your vehicle and then decide whether to be the driver or become a passenger. Sometimes it can be comfortable in the passenger's seat; you might get used to not looking to the future. It is easy to become dependent on others, and lose control of your own destiny.

"They always say that time changes things, but you actually have to change them yourself."
Andy Warhol

In the Disney film "The Lion King", Simba, the young Lion King attempts to avoid adult responsibilities and is challenged by a vision of his father, to make a difference: "Simba, you have forgotten who you are. Look inside yourself. You are more than what you have become."

You might not notice, as time passes, that the comfortable passenger seat has become a comfortable rut. It hurts, but not enough to move. You have to choose whether to increase the strength of your reason why. When the pain of staying in the rut becomes appreciably greater than the pain of getting out of it, then you'll get out of it. If the pleasure of getting out of it is appreciably greater than staying in the rut, you will also get out of it. It's your responsibility; you choose.

"It's not enough to be sick and tired of something, you've got to be sick and tired of being sick and tired; then you'll make a difference."
Andy Gilbert

---

95. Understand Why Others Don't Achieve Goals

24 common reasons why people fail to achieve goals:

- They don't have any goals.
- They have not converted vague aims into specific goals.
- They have not defined any measurement criteria.

- They lack a strong reason why.
- Their goals are not written down.
- They are attempting to change a given.
- They do not plan priorities.
- They are impatient for results.
- They can't visualise it happening.
- They fear change.
- They lack ownership, because the goal has been imposed on them.
- They have no system to reward their achievements.
- They do not check the goal is in harmony with their values.
- They have conflicting goals.
- They word their goals incorrectly i.e. they focus on what they don't want.
- They don't involve others.
- They have too many goals.
- They don't understand or use the power of their subconscious mind.
- They cannot overcome temporary setbacks.
- They lack belief in their own ability.
- They allow others to steal their dream.
- They do not enjoy pursuing the goal.
- They do not take action.
- They do not have a goal that they consider is worthwhile.

TIME TO THINK

So now, you know! Reread the previous list, this time turning each item into a positive way of achieving goals. Take responsibility for what you want to have, do or become, and define your goal. What are you going to choose to do differently?

96. Choose To Make Time

"I haven't got time," is an excuse; a way of saying, "It's not important enough for me, at the moment." It is up to you to choose whether to plan time for those things you say that are important.

John Grisham was a busy lawyer with, "no time to write a book". He chose to get up at 5 a.m. to write his first novel *"A Time to Kill"*. He approached 26 publishers to get it printed and it sold very few copies: 1000 or so. He chose to take responsibility and promote it himself at weekends. There are now over ten million copies in print.

**"The pessimist complains about the wind;
the optimist expects it to change;
the realist adjusts the sails."
William Arthur Ward**

TIME TO REFLECT

**Could I get up earlier each morning?
Could I watch less T.V.?
Could I use spare time more effectively?
Could I read less junk?
Could I give up unimportant/non-urgent tasks?
Could I do something different... if I really wanted to?**

97. Watch Your Language

I sometimes ask participants on Go MAD development programmes a question, "How many of you get up in the morning, sit on the edge of your bed and deliberately say to yourself: 'Today I will get sick, feel ill, be unhappy and fail in everything I do?' " Not surprisingly, people reply that they don't as that would be stupid! I agree with them, and ask the opposite question, "How many of you deliberately give yourself a good ten seconds of positive messages about how successful you will be and how healthy you feel?" At this point, the room normally goes quiet. Many people realise the danger of programming their minds with hindering thoughts, but don't recognise the benefits of choosing to deliberately plant helpful thoughts instead. You have the choice.

**"This is a world of action,
and not for moping and groaning in."
Charles Dickens**

Have you noticed how many people when asked the question, "How are you?" reply, "Not bad," or, "Alright"? Some even reply, "Okay". Very often, their tone of voice is subdued or downbeat. Why not make a difference to yourself and others by saying something like, "Fantastic," or, "Excellent"? A friend of mine, Peter, delights in watching the reaction he gets when he answers, "Brilliant – if life gets any better I'll be amazed!"

**"You must be the change
you wish to see in the world."
Mahatma Gandhi**

Watch out for phrases which start, "I can't", "I should", and "I have to". Take responsibility for stating what you want, or choose to do, rather than implying that someone else is preventing, obliging or forcing you. Use "I" to describe your feelings rather than generalising or hiding behind a collective opinion, i.e. "It is felt…" or, "we all feel that…"

TIME TO THINK

What language do you frequently use that you could consciously change to be more positive?

What words or catch phrases have you got into the habit of saying?

98. Start The Day With Energy

Eliminate negative feelings when they appear by saying, "I'm responsible for the way I feel", and then doing some thing to change it. If ever I wake up in the morning and, as occasionally I do, feel I would rather have a few more minutes sleep, I deliberately choose to say one word. That word is ENERGY! However, I don't just say it to myself, I shout it in an energetic way: EN-ER-GY!!! This works by creating the mental state I want with the words I use. Now at this point I should make you aware that my wife, Harriett, is very understanding (principle five: involve others) and also uses the same method.

TIME TO THINK

You can gain valuable feedback, particularly about your self-belief, from the emotions, you feel in response to your goal. Treat your feelings as feedback by asking:

What is this telling me?

How can I use this information to move forward?

Then take action based on your answers.

99. Choose To Develop Yourself

The aim of this book, in line with my primary aim, is to help you understand and develop your ability to make a difference. However, I can only provide the help; you must develop your own ability.

Taking personal responsibility for doing this means not being dependent on others for providing training and development for you. The concept of *lifelong learning* involves investing your time, and possible money, into developing yourself. It is up to you to make this choice. The people we researched, who consistently Go MAD, all took responsibility for their own development.

"I am still learning."
Michaelangelo

---

100. Go MAD With The Help Of Others

You choose who to involve; how to involve them; when to involve them, and what to involve them in. There is plenty of help available in this world, if you choose to use it.

101. Let Go Of The Past And Move On

Take responsibility for learning from past successes, as well as past mistakes or setbacks – both your own and those of others. It's okay to visit the past; just don't live in it. And if the past hurts: don't re-watch a bad movie. Many people seem too busy replaying their past, that they miss the present and don't spend time creating their future. If you want to Go MAD in the future, you must be willing to let go of the past – after taking the learning with you.

"Learn from yesterday, live for today,
hope for tomorrow.
The important thing is
not to stop questioning."
Albert Einstein

Psychologists have estimated that individuals have approximately 60,000 thoughts each day. However, 90% of these are the same as previous thoughts. These old ways of thinking and acting prevent the new from happening. Negative thoughts can keep out positive ones. Without clearing the junk from the garage there will be no space for the new car.

> **"You can let the past keep hold of you, or you can choose to take hold of the future."**
> **Andy Gilbert**

If it's in the past, choose to react differently. If it is a given, take the learning from it and look forward.

Forgive yourself; tolerate any imperfections; accept yourself as you are, and look to develop. Learn to let go of defending the past.

TIME TO REFLECT

How easily can you say:
* "I was wrong/I made a mistake."
* "I changed my mind."
* "I don't know," or, "I don't know, but I'll find out."

When these three things can be admitted out loud, you will spend less time and energy defending the past. This will increase the time and energy you have available to focus on making a difference in the future.

102. Overcome Bitterness And Resentment

I have met, and continue to meet, people who appear to be so bitter about something – or usually someone or some group – that it impairs their ability to Go MAD. All their energy is taken up reliving negative emotions and experiences – and, of course, programming them deeper in their subconscious mind. These emotions are normally expressed as blame or jealousy, and are a total waste of time.

> **"He who angers you, conquers you."**
> **Buddha**

Feelings of anger, bitterness and resentment are not caused by other people. They are caused by your response to the situation. You can choose your response to any given situation if you take responsibility for your thoughts and actions.

**"Don't go around saying the world owes you a living.
The world owes you nothing. It was here first."
Mark Twain**

A useful question to ask yourself, when encountering such emotions, is: "Is this bigger than me, or am I bigger than this?" Once again, it's your choice!

TIME TO WRITE

Have you heard the phrase: "Learn to forgive and forget"? Well it's quite different from the common interpretation, "I'll say I forgive, but I'll remind myself of it on a regular basis, because I've got nothing more important to focus on!"

Here is an activity to do on a separate piece of paper, which I sometimes refer to as the *baggage removal exercise*.

1. Make a list of people who have upset or hurt you.
2. Write down what you have done to upset or hurt others.
3. Throw the list away or, preferably, burn it.
4. Forgive the offenders (them and you).

103. Be Decisive

Accept what you cannot change and change what you cannot accept. Do what others make excuses about not doing. Vaccinate yourself against procrastination, by being decisive. Decide whether you will or you won't, rather than waste time sitting on the fence.

**Procrastination is the habit of putting off
until the day after tomorrow, what
you could have done the day before yesterday.**

Convert wishful thinking into purposeful, action. Ask high quality questions of yourself in order to gain high quality answers. Take responsibility for making it happen.

104. Commit Yourself To Go MAD

Commitment is one step beyond making a decision. You must first make a decision to Go MAD and then you must make the commitment to do what it takes. Once the first five key principles have been applied, sign the invisible contract that says: "I will do what it takes." There is power in making a commitment. This is the key aspect of taking personal responsibility, which will enable you to maintain momentum. I cannot explain this power more succinctly than the German philosopher, Goethe with his descriptive, and ultimately inspirational, quote.

**"Until one is committed
there is hesitancy,
the chance to draw back,
always ineffectiveness.**

**Concerning all acts of initiative
there is one elementary truth,
the ignorance of which kills
countless ideas and endless plans:
That the moment one definitely commits oneself,
then providence moves too.**

**All sorts of things occur to help one
that would never otherwise have occurred.
A whole stream of events issues from the decision,
raising in one's favour all manner of**

unforeseen incidents and meetings and
material assistance, which no man
could have dreamed would come his way.

Whatever you can do or
dream you can, begin it!
Boldness has genius, power and
magic in it.''
Johann Wolfgang Von Goethe

Reread this quote and note the reference to *providence*. Think of this as the subconscious mind acting on instructions, now that the conscious mind has deliberately committed to doing whatever it takes to Go MAD.

TIME TO REFLECT

Having reached the end of this section, take time to consider the following questions:

What will I take personal responsibility for doing?

What was the most important aspect of Go MAD Principle Six that I realised?

What does taking personal responsibility mean to me?

What are the implications of taking personal responsibility?

What do I want to consider doing differently?

What do I want to continue doing successfully?

**"Continuous improvement is better than
delayed perfection."
Mark Twain**

Principle Seven

TAKE ACTION

AND MEASURE THE

RESULTS

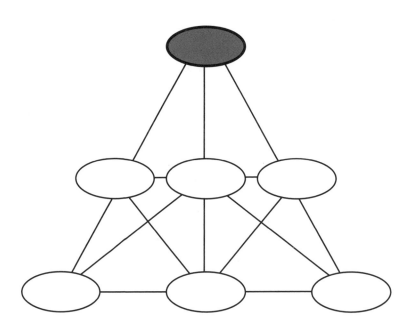

**"It's not the critic who counts;
not the man who points out
how the strong man stumbled,
or where the doer of deeds
could have done better.
The credit belongs to the man
who is actually in the arena,
whose face is marred by dust
and sweat and blood;
who strives valiantly;
who errs and comes short again and again,
who knows the great enthusiasms,
the great devotions and
spends himself in a worthy cause;
who at best knows the triumph
of high achievement;
and who at worst, if he fails,
at least fails while daring greatly,
so that his place shall never be with
those cold and timid souls who know
neither victory nor defeat."
Theodore Roosevelt**

105.   Get Ready, Get Set, Go MAD

You should be ready to take action by now, having applied the first six Go MAD key principles. **NOW** is the time. You've done your personal planning (principles one to three) and you've taken steps to maintain momentum (principles four to six). Now it's time for you to take action; to Go MAD and measure the results.

**"You can't build a reputation
on what you're going to do."
Henry Ford**

Going MAD is beyond knowing how to Go MAD. Being the brightness is one step beyond seeing the light. Don't talk about it – do it! In order to make a difference, you've got to make a start.

Each day has 1440 minutes; start by allocating just 1% – 14 minutes – on the difference you have chosen to make. If you choose not to even do this, you're not serious about making a difference and need to check your application of the other key principles. Never confuse intention, with action.

**"If you wait until the wind
and the weather are just right,
you will never plant anything
and never harvest anything."
Ecclesiastes 11:4**

Start to Go MAD now. Not later, next month or someday – these words often mean never. The Chinese philosopher Lao Tzu, wrote the following words over 2,500 years ago: **"The journey of a thousand miles, starts with a single step."** Their relevance is obvious: take a single step today, however small, and start to Go MAD.

106. Act With Integrity

The difference you choose to make is your decision. How you choose to act and apply the Go MAD key principles is up to you. I hope you apply them to make a difference that benefits yourself and others, without harm to any other person.

**Your reputation is what others think you are;
your credibility is what others know you are;
your integrity is what you know you are.**

You can't have, or act with, a bit of integrity; you either have it, or you don't!

107. Face Challenges

There is no *failure* (section 76), only opportunities to learn. Even with the most detailed of plans, you are still unlikely to identify, or eliminate, all obstacles. See them as *challenges*, as this will be more constructive in helping you to accept them as part of the journey. Being solution focused, you will take responsibility for handling them as they arise, rather than seeing them as an excuse to quit. Keep focused on your goal and reason why.

Winners never quit and quitters never win.

Persist in applying the first six Go MAD principles, whatever challenge you face, and you will succeed. Challenges can often be broken down into smaller elements – like goals and sub-goals. Tackle each of the smaller elements and learn from the experience. Remember that the greatest challenges are those that exist in your mind!

> **"There are costs and risks to a programme of action, but they are far less than the long range risks and costs of comfortable inaction."**
> **John F. Kennedy**

108. Recognise The Difference Between Perseverance And Stubbornness

Winston Churchill, the former British Prime Minster, once gave a speech in a university debate that lasted only a few seconds. He stood up and said, "Never give in, never give in, never, never, never, never," and then sat down again.

> **"I have more respect for the fellow**
> **with a single idea who gets there,**
> **than for the fellow**
> **with a thousand ideas who does nothing."**
> **Thomas Edison**

Perseverance is never giving up in pursuit of your goal, but also being flexible in the way that you do it. On the other hand, stubbornness is ignoring the facts and being unreasonably obstinate about making a difference that cannot be made.

> **If you continue to do what you've continually done, you will continue to get what you've continually got.**

109. Measure The Difference

Keep track of your progress and plan reviews in your diary to ensure this happens. Refer back to your goal, and sub-goals, to ensure you are measuring the specific difference you defined. How you measure the difference is for you to decide. Some things are obviously easier to measure than others, e.g. have certain events happened or not? Measurements of time, cost and quantity are also relatively easy to measure.

An area that some people struggle with is measuring a *softer* developmental goal. For example: increasing confidence or reducing stress. The two easiest ways of doing this are as follows:

- Ask yourself what action you would be able to do as a result of having either increased confidence or reduced stress. Then measure your ability to take this action.

- Assess your current level of confidence or stress on a simple scale of one (low) to ten (high). This is your own internal assessment and not a comparison with anyone else. Decide how high on the scale you would like to increase your confidence to, or how low you would like to reduce your stress to. Then identify your own internal benchmark to measure yourself against. For example, if you want to be a six for confidence, and currently have assessed yourself as a three, have you ever been a six before? In other words, how will you recognise it when you get there? If you have been a six before, then remember what it was like and how it felt in detail. If you haven't been a six before, either imagine what it would be like or identify someone who you consider to be a six. What behaviour do they display that indicates they are a six? What is the behaviour that you want? Define that behaviour and the context in which you want to use it, and use this as your measurement.

TIME TO THINK

Defining measurable goals needs to happen as soon as you have decided to make a difference. If this doesn't happen, it can be very difficult to measure future success. Answering the following questions will help.

> **What is the measurable difference I want?**
>
> **How will I know when I've got it?**
>
> **How will I measure the results?**
>
> **When will I record the results?**
>
> **How will I record the results?**

Have a visual record and reminder of your progress towards your goal. It will help you to continually programme your mind with messages of achievement and success.

110. Define New Goals Before Achieving The Existing Ones

I mentioned earlier about the importance of doing this. Before the end goal is reached, decide what you want to make a difference about next. This could be an extension to the existing goal, which in effect converts the current goal to a sub-goal. Alternatively, you might choose to Go MAD about something completely different.

The purpose of defining new goals is to avoid the feeling of one minute having a worthwhile goal and then having nothing to look forward to once it has been achieved. Your subconscious mind will recognise this and, if you are not careful, your momentum will not be maintained. Your progress will become slower to make the most of enjoying still having a goal to work towards.

111. Have Fun And Enjoy Yourself

If success is the progressive realisation of a worthwhile goal, you can have fun and be happy on the journey towards your destination (refer back to sections 29 and 30); you don't have to wait until you arrive!

Enjoying yourself is optional and you don't have to do it. In which case certainly don't include it in your plan of important priorities. You might even want to consider not involving those who enjoy making a difference, just in case they cause it to be fun for everyone! If Going MAD seems like hard work to you, remember you can develop a different self-belief by returning to principle four and deciding to Go MAD about having fun!

112. Celebrate Success

It's obvious, so just do it. Remember to acknowledge the help of others involved and include them in your success celebrations, whatever they might be.

"Rest satisfied with doing well, and leave others to talk of you as they will."
Pythagoras

TIME TO REFLECT

That's it, the end – or very nearly. Just take a few moments to consider the following questions:

What was the most important aspect of Go MAD Principle Seven that I realised?

What are the implications?

Which of the seven Go MAD key principles do I need to understand more fully?

Which of the seven Go MAD key principles am I naturally good at applying?

What else do I want to consider making a difference about?

What, if anything, is preventing me from making a difference?

What will I do about it?

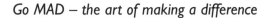

> "I cannot motivate you, and you cannot motivate me, for it means to take over each other's freedom. I cannot choose for you and you cannot choose for me. It follows from this simple truth that the only way I can stimulate your motivation is to create an environment in which that would be for you the logical choice."
> **Peter Koestenbaum**

Go MAD About Thinking

APPLYING GO MAD AS A

SOLUTION FOCUSED

THINKING SYSTEM

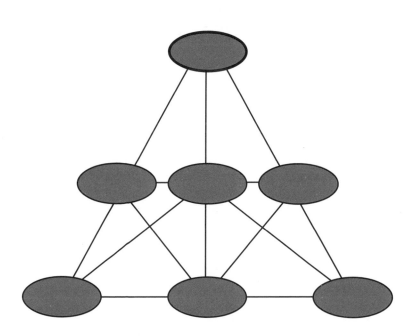

**"We think so little that when we do
we call it creativity."
Voltaire**

113. Thinking About Thinking

When I use the word "thinking", I mean the thoughts that go through your mind. Sometimes thoughts will pop into your head as ideas, memories or questions – perhaps unexpectedly – and then disappear again. At other times you might find yourself consciously thinking about an issue, or attempting to solve a problem, that is going round and round inside your head, which you are seemingly unable to escape from. Imagining the future and day dreaming are also forms of thinking, as there is something going through your mind – even if you are not fully conscious of doing it.

"You cannot always control your circumstances, but you can always control your own thoughts."
Charles E. Popplestone

In order to review the effectiveness of your thinking it is necessary to become consciously aware of not just what you are thinking, but also of how you are thinking. Of course, you could just measure the results you get as a consequence of taking action (principle seven). However, your actions will be based upon the quality of your thinking, so if your actions are not getting the desired results then you need to revisit your thinking and understand which components you want to change.

Now, whilst this might appear common sense I realise that for most people this is easier said (or written) than done. Hence, the purpose of this section of the book is to help you understand the broadest application of Go MAD – as a thinking system – to help yourself and others achieve even greater success.

"Your thoughts lead to actions which lead to results. Therefore the key to a successful outcome is the quality of thinking which precedes the action you take."
Andy Gilbert

---

114. The Four Go MAD Thinking Components

My ongoing quest to explain complex issues in a straightforward manner often provides challenges, especially when dealing with people who enjoy complexity and detailed theory for the sake of it. So I take heart from the following wise words:

"Everything should be made as simple as possible, but not simpler."
Albert Einstein

When you think to yourself, your thoughts will either help or hinder your progress towards your defined goal. Your thinking is comprised of various elements which combine in a sequence unique to your experience and view of the world. I refer to these as the Four Go MAD Thinking Components i.e. the four things which you do in your head that most help or hinder your ability to make a difference and achieve results. I consider these to be equally as important as the Seven Go MAD Key Principles and crucial to understand if you are seeking to attain or maintain a continued level of high performance in your life.

In simple terms your thoughts are comprised of two elements – what you say to yourself and what you focus on. When you talk to yourself (inside your head) you will be either asking questions e.g. "What is the easiest way to do this?" (helpful) and, "What's the point?" (hindering), or making statements e.g. "This is exciting" (helpful), "I'll never do it" (hindering), and, "It's too cold" (possibly helpful or hindering depending on the context). These statements are most likely to relate to three things: you and your ability; other people and how they affect you; and the situation or environment.

"It is our attitude at the beginning of a difficult undertaking which, more than anything else, will determine its successful outcome."
William James

When thinking, your focus will either be on the past e.g. recalling a past success (helpful) or an unpleasant memory (hindering), or on the future e.g. imagining a positive, pleasant outcome (helpful) or things going wrong (hindering).

So, in summary the Four Go MAD Thinking Components (in no particular order) are:

1. Statements you make to yourself about yourself, others and/or the situation
2. Questions you ask yourself
3. Memories of the past you recall
4. Future outcomes you imagine

TIME TO THINK

Identify a situation that is bothering you and ask yourself the following questions:

"What am I saying to myself about either myself, others or this situation?"

"What questions am I asking myself?"

"What memories am I recalling?"

"What future am I imagining?"

Identify which components are helpful and which are hindering.

**"If there's a way to do it better... find it."
Thomas Edison**

If the thought you are having is helpful... great! If the thought you are having is hindering, or likely to hinder, your progress towards making a difference, ask yourself the following question, phrasing it appropriately, relevant to the hindering component:

"If I was to focus on something more helpful, what could I possibly say, ask, recall or imagine that would help me move forward?"

Repeat the new helpful thinking component in your mind several times. Repetition causes a habit to form. This repetition of new helpful thinking components is particularly important to replace previous hindering thoughts. You might need to remind yourself with a trigger (see page 45) to reinforce this.

115. Take Personal Responsibility For Your Thoughts

In January 2004 an interesting incident happened on a development programme I was leading. One of the participants, a senior manager called Jane, asked if I would help her with her thinking about a difficult personal situation which was hindering her progress with the task the group was focused on. She was visibly distressed and stated that her head was filled with hindering thoughts about her husband who had been diagnosed terminally ill with cancer. Jane told me that there was no point in thinking helpful thoughts because of her situation (hindering statement), it would be terrible without him (hindering imagined future) and why did it have to happen? (hindering question).

**"Since we cannot change reality,
let us change the eyes which see reality."
Niko Kazantzakis**

Being sensitive to the longer-term emotional impact of her situation, yet seeking to help her short-term thinking, I invited Jane to think about doing something in the immediate future which she could imagine her husband would enjoy. She thought about this and decided to take him for a meal at the weekend. I asked her what the most helpful questions were that she could ask herself and she replied, "Where could we go?" and, "Which friends shall we invite?" Jane then suddenly remembered a great restaurant where they had previously enjoyed a meal and stated, "I know where to go, it's got a fantastic atmosphere and we will have a great meal!" I commented to her that she was doing some helpful thinking in order to make a difference and achieve a goal of enjoying time with her husband whilst he was alive. Jane looked at me and said, "I get it; this Go MAD thinking stuff isn't about making things right; it's about me taking responsibility for the choices I have."

"Heal the past, live the present, dream the future."
Mary Engelbreit

---

116. Adopting A Solution Focused Approach To Your Thinking

Everyone has problems of one sort or another. The question is whether or not you choose to allow the problem to dominate your thinking or you choose to go in search of solutions. Developing awareness of how you apply the Four Go MAD Thinking Components and then choosing to change hindering thoughts into helpful ones is a critical success factor in life. Day-to-day the easiest way to do this is to simply ask yourself on a regular basis, "Is this helpful or hindering?" Then take action, as appropriate.

A solution focused approach to thinking comprises three stages:

1. Identify what works and keep doing it (i.e. the helpful thinking and actions which lead to the results you want).
2. Identify what doesn't work and change it (i.e. the hindering thinking and actions which don't lead to the results you want).
3. Use a success based thinking system to develop high performance thinking on a consistent basis. (The Go MAD Framework is an example of a thinking system based upon the key success principles of making a difference.)

"No problem can withstand the assault of sustained thinking."
Voltaire

---

117. Systems Thinking v Process Thinking

Imagine you wanted to cook a fabulous dinner for friends or guests and you had clearly visualised your defined goal about having a great evening. As part of your possibility thinking you considered what dishes to cook and decided to test a new recipe for the main course. Having never prepared this dish before, you decide to follow precisely the detailed recipe instructions. With exactly the right ingredients and utensils, you prepare and cook the food in accordance with the guidance. You follow the process and you get great results – it even looks similar to the picture in the recipe book!

"Success is a science;
if you have the conditions, you get the results."
Oscar Wilde

However, cooking the main course is only one part of the bigger picture. There is also the need to consider the starter, dessert, drinks, welcoming guests, table layout, seating plan, after dinner entertainment and perhaps more. All these elements will combine and contribute to achieving the desired outcome. Unfortunately, in life, there isn't a recipe or process to follow to guarantee the outcome you desire. Instead, you have to take action and keep an eye on all these elements, understanding how they relate and impact on each other as part of a larger "system".

So, **process thinking** is where you follow a chronological order of thoughts – maybe asking certain questions in the same sequence – in order to achieve a specific outcome, i.e. "If I do A, B, C and D, I will achieve XYZ." **Systems thinking**, on the other hand, is where you identify the key elements which are essential to the larger system and understand the relationships between them, i.e. "In order to achieve XYZ I need to consider how to handle A, B, C and D elements, knowing that the actions I take on one element will impact on the other elements."

"Great things are not done by impulse, but by a series of small things brought together."
Vincent Van Gogh

The Go MAD Framework brings together seven key elements of success. Whilst you can assess, develop or take action on one or two of these elements, if you ignore the remaining five or six the probability of being successful will be dramatically reduced.

Look at the Go MAD Framework as a system rather than a process. This book focuses on helping you to understand the key elements of the system; the next step is to understand how they link together.

118. Systems Thinking And Thinking Systems

There are many different types of system, for example: mechanical systems (e.g. a car), ecological systems (e.g. a river estuary), biological systems (e.g. the human body) and people systems (e.g. a family or team).

TIME TO THINK

Select one of the above examples of a system and identify the key elements of it. Then imagine changing a significant aspect of that element. What impact would it have on another element within the system? What might the further impact of this be on the other elements?

By considering the whole rather than just one part you are now engaging in systems thinking. By the way, how aware were you of the Four Go MAD Thinking Components during that exercise? Notice how I influenced two of them by asking you questions and instructing you to use your imagination. If you did this thinking exercise, what were you saying to yourself and possibly remembering?

"Your life is what your thoughts make it."
Marcus Aurelius

Another type of system is a thinking system. By combining the Go MAD Thinking Components with the Go MAD Framework you can think systemically, considering the relationships between all the elements necessary to make a difference. By engaging your imagination and asking yourself high quality questions relevant to each part of the Go MAD Framework, you will develop your thinking in a helpful way. Understanding the relationship links between the initial six Go MAD key principles will enhance your ability to take action (principle seven) in a solution focused way and enable you to adjust your thinking, when necessary, as a consequence of measuring the results you achieve.

Go MAD is a solution focused thinking system which enables people to take a systems thinking approach to achieving success by considering the key elements, individually and as a holistic framework to make a measurable difference.

---

119. Think About The Links In The Go MAD Framework

A key aspect of taking personal responsibility (principle six) is to understand the choices you have in relation to the other elements in the system. These are presented on the next page in the form of questions designed to help you think.

1. Reason Why:
   - Can I be bothered? (Yes or no).
   - How much responsibility will I take?

**"If you choose not to decide,
you still have made a choice."
Neil Peart**

---

2. Define Goal:
   - What specific difference do I choose to make?
   - What will I do to more clearly define what I want to achieve?
   - How will I measure my success and by what date?

3. Plan Priorities:
   - How much time do I choose to spend exploring possibilities?
   - Which possibilities do I choose as my priorities?
   - How much time will I plan in my diary to work towards achieving my priorities?

4. Self-Belief:
   - What will I do to increase my confidence?
   - Which development activities do I choose to undertake in order to gain increased knowledge or skills?
   - Which hindering thoughts do I choose to change to more helpful ones?

5. Involving Others:
   - Who will I choose to involve to support me?
   - How will I choose to ask for help?
   - When will I involve them?

**"A prudent question is one-half of wisdom."
Francis Bacon**

Notice how the phraseology of the question focuses your mind towards making decisions and choices. The higher the quality of the question you ask yourself, the more effective your thinking will be.

For a more detailed understanding about how to design and ask high quality questions to help yourself and others with solution focused thinking I suggest reading "Go MAD About Coaching" by Andy Gilbert and Ian Chakravorty. This book explains the framework links and how to use the Go MAD Thinking System in a lot more detail.

In addition to the choice lines, which link Personal Responsibility with the initial five elements of the thinking system, there are an additional six critical links to consider. These form two triangles which are explained in the following chapters.

120. Develop A Strong Internal Triangle

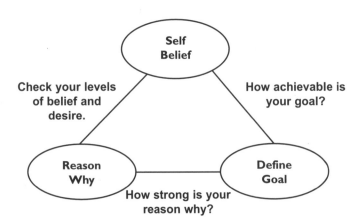

This triangle highlights the importance of the softer "internal" issues relating to making a difference and encompasses motivation, confidence, values, feelings, aspirations and vision. In other words, the stuff that is normally hidden from others and kept to yourself. Without a strong internal triangle it is pointless to involve others or plan priorities.

Consider the impact if you don't have sufficient desire, confidence or clarity about the difference you want to make. How can you involve others or plan if you don't know what you want? How likely are you to take action and measure results if you haven't got a strong enough reason to make a difference?

121. Explore And Plan The External Triangle

The external triangle comprises the more tangible factors which are easier to see, touch and have "external" hard evidence of. It includes objectives, ideas, tasks, priorities, plans, timescales, logistics and people.

The link between the defined goal and involving others is referred to as the "buy-in" line and, together with involving others and tasks, is one of the ten Go MAD possibility thinking areas (see section 54) to be explored before planning priorities.

From a systems thinking perspective, it is easy to recognise that if the goal is redefined, for any reason or at any point, this will affect the plan which will need to be reprioritised, perhaps after further possibility thinking, and different people will need to be influenced to do specific tasks. This could well affect your self-belief and you might need to strengthen your internal triangle.

122. Apply Go MAD Thinking At Four Levels

It is easy to think that Go MAD is all about increasing your personal effectiveness and ability to achieve results – which it is. However, this one level of application is really only the tip of the iceberg.

Since 1998 the number and variety of uses for Go MAD as a thinking system has dramatically grown. The applications broadly fall under the four headings in the above diagram. The following four chapters provide a brief insight into each of these applications.

123. Level One: Personal Effectiveness (Your Thinking)

As an individual, you can use the Go MAD Thinking System to analyse the past, diagnose or assess the present, and develop the future.

TIME TO REFLECT

Remember a situation where you set out to achieve something and, for whatever reason, were unsuccessful. Now use the Go MAD Framework to analyse which of the key elements was missing or weaker. How strong was your internal triangle? How well did you involve others or obtain their buy-in? How effectively did you plan your priorities? To what extent did you take personal responsibility for making it happen?

"It is never too late to be what you might have been."
George Elliot

Imagine, towards the end of your life, looking back at your achievements and the differences you made at home and work. How effective were you in taking personal responsibility for the differences that were most important to you? Which of the Go MAD Key Principles could you have been more effective in applying?

The good news is that you don't have to wait that long! By applying the Go MAD Thinking System as a diagnostic tool you can assess your current activities, identify which elements would benefit from further development and then take appropriate action. You might even want to review your current activities, reprioritise them and park those where your reason why is not strong enough. This is a great way to save time and money!

"We must not, in trying to think about how we can make a big difference, ignore the small daily differences we can make, which, over time, add up to big differences that we often cannot foresee."
Marian Wright Edelman

As a development framework, Go MAD can be used to systematically think and take action on the elements essential to making a measurable difference. Engage the Four Go MAD Thinking Components to:

1. Ask yourself high quality questions about each of the Seven Key Success Principles and how they interact in the context of your goal.
2. Talk internally to yourself in a helpful manner about moving forward and the situation you face.
3. Remember experiences and past events you can draw upon and learn from.
4. Imagine your desired goal with absolute clarity and vivid detail.

Here is an example of a typical realisation:

> **"Go MAD is a system of thinking that really gets you thinking in a way that can enrich both your personal and business life."**
> **Jonathan Donovan, Head of Employee Relations, O$_2$**

---

124. Level Two: Coaching Others (Their Thinking)

In simple terms, coaching is one person helping another person with their thinking. The key to this is to ask helpful high quality questions which engage the imagination when defining goals and exploring possibilities; focus the mind when planning priorities and committing to take personal responsibility; and enable the person to think in a solution focused way.

By controlling the structure, pace and sequence of the questions a Go MAD Coach influences the thinking process of the other person, skilfully guiding them to the appropriate element of the Go MAD Thinking System. Without requiring any knowledge of the coaching content it is very easy for people with good questioning skills and understanding of the Go MAD Framework to help almost anyone increase the probability of their success.

Every two months I lead a Solution Focused Thinking Skills Development Programme for 12 business leaders and managers from a variety of organisations. Last month the youngest person on the programme was helping a much older and experienced Managing Director (who earns nearly 20 times more in salary) with his thinking through the use of the Go MAD Framework. The subject was a complex business issue which the coach knew nothing about, yet despite this she helped him to identify over 40 possibilities and develop a prioritised action plan. It was no surprise to me, but a real thrill to her, when he thanked her with the comment, "That was great – you have really helped me with my thinking!"

125. Level Three: Projects, Meetings and Team Development

Have you ever attended a meeting where the participants don't really want to be there (low reason why), the goal is unclear, the commonly held belief is that nothing will change, someone proposes an idea which is accepted because no other possibilities are explored, no-one takes responsibility for an agreed action and so nothing happens?

Well maybe your meetings are not that disastrous, but perhaps they could be more effective if the person leading the meeting and the participants understood and applied a shared thinking system.

Involving others is one key element of the Go MAD Framework. So where groups of people are working together in teams or on projects it makes sense to ensure they share the same clearly defined goal, which they believe to be achievable and have a strong enough reason to keep motivated towards achieving. It also helps if they have a range of tools and techniques to undertake a variety of possibility thinking, prioritising and planning activities which enable people to get involved in key tasks and take personal responsibility for making a difference.

Once again, the Go MAD Thinking System can be easily applied to analyse the effectiveness of past projects, review current projects or team progress and develop higher performance in the future. If you are interested in making a difference in these areas, I recommend you read, "How to Save Time and Money by Managing Meetings Effectively" by Andy Gilbert and Graham Field, which contains 101 practical tips.

Here is an example of a measurable difference:

"I want everyone to know how delighted I and the 3M UK Commercial, Consumer and Office business team have been with the learning and application of the Go MAD Thinking System. It has provided us with the missing links to the team's enhanced effectiveness and a common vocabulary to deal with complex issues. The team embraced the system straight away and applied it to the submission of aggressive growth plans to our European and USA Executive Management. They were so pleased with our submissions that we secured over fifty percent of the total investment funding available to the whole of Europe."
Geoff Tabbner, Country Business Leader, 3M

---

126. Level Four: Leadership Thinking And Cultural Transformation

Imagine if everyone who worked in an organisation shared the same thinking system, with an easy to understand language, aligned to clearly defined business goals. It makes sense! If everyone is equipped to use the same IT system, why not equip people to use the same thinking system?

In addition to my research and writing activities, much of my time is spent working with leaders in organisations developing business improvement and leadership thinking programmes to enable business results to be achieved quicker and more cost effectively. As you might expect, achieving large-scale change can often be quite complex.

"The old guard in any society resents new methods, for old guards wear the decorations and medals won by waging battle in the old accepted manner."
Martin Luther King, Jnr

From 2000 onwards, the team of Go MAD Thinking Engineers have developed and tested ways of embedding Go MAD as a thinking system using a rigorous installation methodology to guarantee measurable results. The Go MAD Thinking System, which you have become familiar with in this book, has been developed into the Go MAD Organisational Development Framework to analyse and facilitate change at a macro level.

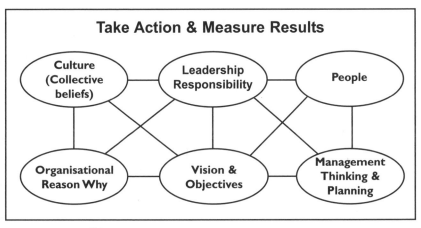

Go MAD® Organisational Development Framework

So, instead of Personal Responsibility this becomes Leadership Responsibility; the People involved include employees, customers and other stakeholders; the goal becomes the Vision; the individual Self-Belief becomes the Culture of the organisation; the Reason Why becomes an Organisational Reason Why (e.g. shareholder value); and Planning Priorities becomes a Management Thinking activity in line with the business objectives and direction given by the leadership team.

Adopting a systems thinking approach to organisational change means that we need to consider the individual elements and their impact upon each other. Potentially there will be a need to take action and measure the results of each element. A different set of questions can now be asked to analyse the macro differences leaders are seeking to make and identify weaknesses in the system.

- What is the organisational reason for seeking change?
- What is the leadership vision?
- How strong is the existing culture to support the vision?
- How is the vision being communicated to managers responsible for the planning and implementation?
- How effectively are the objectives being communicated to other people (employees, customers, suppliers,etc.) to obtain their commitment?

Here is an example of what can be achieved:

"We felt Go MAD was going to be a two-year programme where we were going to fundamentally change the whole culture within our organisation. The results are fantastic. We've seen a significant shift in the levels of customer satisfaction and the feedback we are getting is fantastic. We've seen a fundamental shift in our employee satisfaction levels and we are also seeing a significant improvement in our shareholders' returns.

We have got tremendous confidence that what we have got in place is the right thing and we are looking at the future with tremendous confidence. I've seen people transform in our organisation. The results for us are what are important and we are absolutely seeing that in

our company. I don't have any hesitation in giving my commendation and recommendation that people use Go MAD Thinking."
Michael Gould, Managing Director Operations, Aon Employee Benefits

---

Now I realise that this might all seem a bit much if you only want to apply Go MAD Thinking at a personal effectiveness level. However, there might be a time when your reason why is sufficiently strong to help others, and possibly an organisation, make a greater difference. If that time is now, I recommend you read "How to Make A Difference by Transforming Managers into Leaders", by Andy Gilbert & Sally Fagan and, "How to Save Time and Money by Managing Organisational Change Effectively", by Andy Gilbert.

If you are a business leader seeking to make a difference and require further information, contact the Go MAD team and we will send you a free DVD of case-study information (email: info@gomadthinking.com).

"Your legacy should be that you made it better than it was when you got it."
Lee Iacocca

"It is not the strongest of the species that survive,
nor the most intelligent,
but the ones most responsive to change."
Charles Darwin

Final Thoughts

THE BIT AT

THE END

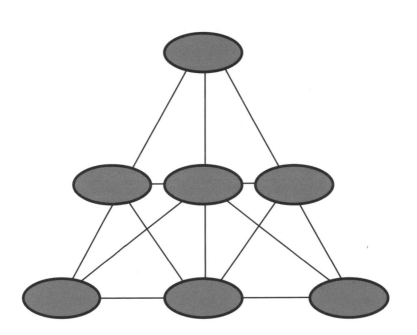

**"One's philosophy is not best expressed in words,
it's expressed in the choices one makes.
In the long run, we shape our lives and we shape
ourselves.
The process never ends until we die.
And the choices we make are ultimately our
responsibility."
Eleanor Roosevelt**

127. You've Read The Book, Now Make The Difference!

I wrote this book with the hope that you will choose to apply the Go MAD key principles, not just read about them. The difference between the ordinary and the extraordinary is that little bit *extra* that people have who Go MAD. It sometimes takes that little bit extra to apply the key principles and make the difference. The following quote is from a Managing Director we interviewed and filmed, who summed this up very passionately.

> **"The difference between those that do
> and those that don't,
> is those that are prepared to have a go.
> And really have a go, despite the obstacles."**
> **Simon Ashton**

TIME TO THINK

Are you prepared to have a go? If so, here is a final exercise for you. Imagine in five years time someone was going to give a speech in recognition of the differences that you had made, and present an award to you, for your achievements. What would you like them to say you have done?

128. Challenge Yourself In Three Ways

On many of my development programmes, I include a 90 day Go MAD challenge. This challenge involves applying all the seven Go MAD key principles to make a measurable difference about something that each individual feels strongly about. The differences are then measured at the end of 90 days. Examples of differences made vary considerably; from cost savings of several hundred thousand pounds to developing the confidence to speak in a small group.

I have three challenges for you. However, you must identify if your reason why is strong enough to accept them. If you are not willing to do this, there is nothing further I can do to help.

THE FIRST CHALLENGE

Identify a small, but significant, difference you could make today that would be a step in the right direction towards something you value as important. Take that step.

> **"I am only one, but still I am one;**
> **I cannot do everything, but still I can do something;**
> **I will not refuse to do the something I can do."**
> **Helen Keller**

THE SECOND CHALLENGE

Put a reminder in your diary to do two things. The first of these is to review your progress and measure the results of the actions you have taken towards your goals. Go on, actually pick a date and commit to spend time doing this. Secondly, diarise to reread all or part of this book in the future. Because you will have moved forward and are likely to experience different situations, you will gain new insights from different parts of the book. Certain key principles, which might not be important to you now, might be of greater significance at a later date.

THE THIRD CHALLENGE

If you decide not to apply the content of this book, then learn to live without complaining. The key to this, is learning to accept and love yourself for who you are – which might, of course, involve making a difference! Either way, give the whining dog a rest.

129. Action Planning

What will I do? (actions)	By when? (date)

Goal:

Reasons why I want to achieve this goal:
1.
2.
3.
4.
5.

Possible Challenges/Obstacles:	Solutions:
1.	
2.	
3.	
4.	
5.	

Sub-goals & Actions:	Target Date	Date Achieved
1.		
2.		
3.		
4.		
5.		
6.		
7.		

Date by which goal will be achieved:
Self-Belief Statement 1.
Self-Belief Statement 2.

I am committed to following this plan and take personal responsibility for making any adjustments necessary until I achieve my goal.

Signed .... Date..................

130. Further Information And Resources

If you liked the practical style of this book, and are interested in reading further publications written by myself and the Go MAD team, you might want to consider the following:

**How to Make A Difference by
Transforming Managers into Leaders**
(255 practical tips and ideas to develop your leadership ability.)

**How to Save Time and Money by
Managing Organisational Change Effectively**
(A practical guide to help managers handle people's reaction to organisational change)

**How to Save Time and Money by
Managing Meetings Effectively**
(101 ways to make a difference before, during and after meetings.)

Go MAD About Coaching (plus audio CD)
(Over 200 powerful coaching questions, plus tips, tools, techniques and templates. The manager's guide for helping others to make a difference.)

How to Win in Negotiations
(130 practical tips for preparing and conducting successful negotiations.)

Who's Driving Your Bus?
(An easy to read, inspirational story about the power of the Go MAD Thinking System.)

Go To Work On Your Career
(256 pages of tips, tools and techniques to help manage and develop your career.)

Go MAD – the art of making a difference

Contagious Customer Care
(Easy to read case-studies and practical tips about making a difference.)

59 Minutes to a Calmer Life
(Helpful insights to help reduce stress in your professional and personal life.)

Small Business Big Difference
(Over 200 tested and proven ideas for growing and managing a small to medium-sized business.)

Brain Magic (Book and 6 CD Audio Set)
(Just how does your brain work? 150 of the most commonly asked questions are answered giving you practical tips to living a longer, happier and healthier life)

To order, or register for our free e-zine, simply visit our website at www.gomadthinking.com or telephone +44 (0)1509 891313.

If you are seeking to make a difference within an organisation and would like to have a discussion about any aspect of applying Go MAD as a catalyst for cultural change, leadership thinking, business improvement or management development then please contact one of the Go MAD Thinking Engineers.

Go MAD Research & Consulting Group
Pocket Gate Farm
Off Breakback Road
Woodhouse Eaves
Leicestershire
LE12 8RS

email: info@gomadthinking.com

NOTES

NOTES